Divided Cities

D1082254

Richard Scholar is University Lecturer in French and Fellow of Oriel College, Oxford. He is the author of *The Je-Ne-Sais-Quoi in Early Modern Europe: Encounters with a Certain Something* (OUP, 2005).

The Oxford Amnesty Lectures is a registered charity. Its purpose is to raise funds to increase awareness of Amnesty International in the academic and wider communities. It is otherwise independent of Amnesty International. It began as a fund-raising project for the local Amnesty group in Oxford, and is now one of the world's leading name-lecture series. To date, Oxford Amnesty Lectures has raised around £100,000 for Amnesty International.

Divided Cities

The Oxford Amnesty Lectures 2003

Edited by

Richard Scholar

OXFORD
UNIVERSITY PRESS

OXFORD
UNIVERSITY PRESS

Great Clarendon Street, Oxford OX2 6DP

Oxford University Press is a department of the University of Oxford.
It furthers the University's objective of excellence in research, scholarship,
and education by publishing worldwide in

Oxford New York

Auckland Cape Town Dar es Salaam Hong Kong Karachi
Kuala Lumpur Madrid Melbourne Mexico City Nairobi
New Delhi Shanghai Taipei Toronto

With offices in

Argentina Austria Brazil Chile Czech Republic France Greece
Guatemala Hungary Italy Japan Poland Portugal Singapore
South Korea Switzerland Thailand Turkey Ukraine Vietnam

Oxford is a registered trade mark of Oxford University Press
in the UK and in certain other countries

Published in the United States
by Oxford University Press Inc., New York

© Oxford Amnesty Lectures 2006

British Library Cataloguing in Publication Data

Data available

Library of Congress Cataloging in Publication Data

Data available

Typeset by RefineCatch Limited, Bungay, Suffolk
Printed in Great Britain
on acid-free paper by
Clays Ltd., St Ives plc

ISBN 0–19–280708–0 (Pbk.)   978–0–19–280708–3 (Pbk.)

1

Preface

These lectures were originally given in Oxford in January and February 2003. The lecturers—Patrick Declerck, Stuart Hall, David Harvey, Richard Rogers, Patricia Williams, and James Wolfensohn—were given the opportunity to develop and revise their texts in the light of the points and questions offered by the audience after the lectures. I am grateful to all six of them for coming to speak in Oxford, and for allowing us to publish their lectures in aid of Amnesty International. Peter Hall and Michael Likosky agreed to write responses to the lectures: they have my thanks. So too do those who introduced the speakers or wrote introductions to individual lectures. They are James Attlee, Alan Budd, Stephen Howe, Maria Kaika, Martin Kemp, Sebastian Mallaby, Ceri Peach, Jane Shaw, and Erik Swyngedouw. Many people in and outside Oxford, too numerous to mention here, offered further practical help and assistance of various kinds: I thank them warmly. In 2003, for the first time, Oxford Amnesty Lectures teamed up with two other of the city's institutions—Modern Art Oxford and the Phoenix Picturehouse—to stage a private viewing and a season of films in conjunction with the lectures. Our thanks are due to both institutions for their participation in these events. Without the hard work of the other members of the Oxford Amnesty Lectures committee, there would have been no lectures, no events, and no book. They are Tim Chesters, Melissa McCarthy, Chris Miller, Nicholas Owen, Fabienne Pagnier, Deana Rankin, Stephen Shute, Kate Tunstall, and Wes Williams.

R.W.S.

Contents

Contributors

JAMES ATTLEE works at Tate Publishing, London, and is the author, with Lisa Le Feuvre, of *Gordon-Matta-Clark: The Space Between* (2002).

PATRICK DECLERCK is a psychoanalyst and philosopher, co-founder of the first counselling and medical service for the homeless in France, and the author of *Les Naufragés* (The Shipwrecked) (2001), a prize-winning study of homelessness in Paris.

PETER HALL is Professor of Planning at the Bartlett School of Architecture and Planning, University College London, and the author of *Cities in Civilization* (1998).

STUART HALL is Emeritus Professor of Sociology at The Open University. His works include *Questions of Cultural Identity* (1996) and *Stuart Hall: Critical Dialogues in Cultural Studies* (1996).

DAVID HARVEY is Distinguished Professor at the CUNY Graduate Center, New York, and the author of many works including *Social Justice and the City* (1973), *The Condition of Postmodernity* (1989), and *The New Imperialism* (2003).

STEPHEN HOWE is Tutor in Politics at Ruskin College, Oxford, and the author of *Ireland and Empire* (2000) and *Empire: A Very Short Introduction* (2002).

MARIA KAIKA is an architect, University Lecturer in Urban Geography and Fellow of St Edmund Hall, Oxford, and the author of *City of Flows: Water, Modernity, and the City* (2004).

CONTRIBUTORS

MICHAEL B. LIKOSKY is Lecturer in International Economic Law in the Law Department of the School of Oriental and African Studies (SOAS), University of London, and the author of *The Silicon Empire: Law, Culture and Commerce* (2005).

SEBASTIAN MALLABY is a *Washington Post* columnist and the author of a book about James Wolfensohn, *The World's Banker: Failed States, Financial Crises, and the Wealth and Poverty of Nations* (2004).

RICHARD ROGERS is the architect of many buildings including the Pompidou Centre (Paris) and the Lloyds Building (London). A Labour peer, he is also Chief Adviser on Architecture and Urbanism to the Mayor of London and the author of the Urban Task Force Report on British cities, 'Towards an Urban Renaissance' (1999).

RICHARD SCHOLAR is University Lecturer in French and a Fellow of Oriel College, Oxford. He is the author of *The Je-Ne-Sais-Quoi in Early Modern Europe: Encounters with a Certain Something* (2005).

JANE SHAW is Dean of Divinity, Chaplain, and Fellow of New College, Oxford.

ERIK SWYNGEDOUW is University Reader in Economic Geography and Fellow of St Peter's College, Oxford.

PATRICIA J. WILLIAMS is Professor of Law at Columbia University, a BBC Reith Lecturer, and a MacArthur Fellow. She is a columnist for *The Nation* and the author of *The Alchemy of Race and Rights* (1991), *Seeing a Color-Blind Future* (1997), and *Open House* (2004).

JAMES D. WOLFENSOHN was President of the World Bank from 1995 until May 2005.

Introduction

Richard Scholar

On a quiet corner of the rue des Écoles, a street close to the Sorbonne in the heart of Paris's Latin Quarter, there stands today a statue of the sixteenth-century humanist, Michel de Montaigne, whose essays were read by Shakespeare and remain a landmark of European literature and thought. The statue is clearly intended to celebrate not only one of France's great intellectuals, but also Paris itself, for beneath the seated figure of Montaigne are lines which read like a love-letter to the city:

I do not want to forget this, that I never rebel so much against France as not to regard Paris with a friendly eye; she has had my heart since my childhood [. . .] I am a Frenchman only by this great city: great in population, great in the felicity of her situation, but above all great and incomparable in the variety and diversity of the good things of life; the glory of France, and one of the noblest ornaments of the world.

These lines, taken from Montaigne's third book of *Essays* (first published in 1588), acquire a sense of visceral urgency when one reads them in their context. In the 1580s, the long-running conflict between Catholic and Protestant extremists was tearing France apart, and Paris, a focal point of the conflict, was a divided city. This Montaigne makes clear in the sentence which, while it does not appear among the lines inscribed on his statue in the rue des Écoles, directly follows them in the text: 'May God', he says, invoking the

God worshipped by Catholics and Protestants alike, 'drive our divisions far from her!'[1]

The passage inscribed on Montaigne's statue, when it is completed by the sentence just quoted, provides a fitting epigraph to this book. Divided cities are the stage upon which fundamental political concepts—such as those of citizenship, democracy, and human rights—both find their origins and encounter their limits. Cities are some of the noblest ornaments of the human world because they are made and remade by many people of different kinds gathering in one place to organize a collective existence free from arbitrary violence. The result, at best, is a union of citizens, all sharing equal burdens, duties, opportunities, and rights, in an environment able to accommodate 'the variety and diversity of the good things of life'. It is no surprise then that the city-state (or *polis*) has long provided utopian thinkers with a setting for their accounts of the ideal human society. Yet, all too often, it seems that the cities in which people actually live are a long way from utopia. They are marked not by vital diversity and difference but by divisions that separate the powerful and privileged from those who, for various reasons, suffer deprivation and injustice. Such divisions may take many forms—religious, ethnic, political, economic, social, and psychological—but what all have in common is that they make a genuine union of citizens impossible to maintain. Like Montaigne, we should not admire cities for the good things they make possible without acknowledging the divisions that threaten their well-being and even, at times, their existence.

This book, like the 2003 Oxford Amnesty Lectures on which it is based, takes as its subject neither the late sixteenth-century Paris described by Montaigne, nor the cities of ancient Athens and Rome that he and his contemporaries admired, but the divided cities of the twenty-first century. Three forces at work in today's world make a contemporary examination of the topic vital: urbanization, globalization, and migration. We live in a rapidly urbanizing world. A century ago, roughly a tenth of the world's population lived in cities; by 2050, that figure will have reached 75 per cent. Much of that growth is taking place in the slums of cities in the developing world: according to the United Nations, 1 billion people—32 per cent of the global urban population—currently live in slums, and this figure is set to double in the next thirty years if no serious action is taken.[2] Two forces are conditioning the way in which the world urbanizes: globalization and migration. Globalization, the subject of an earlier volume of Oxford Amnesty Lectures,[3] is best defined here in political and economic terms as the rapid acceleration of exchange in recent decades between peoples, governments, and corporations. Of migration, the subject of a forthcoming volume of Oxford Amnesty Lectures,[4] all that needs to be observed here is that its consequences are being felt mainly in the world's ever-expanding cities. Urbanization, globalization, and migration are massive and interrelated forces that affect the nature and extent of human rights and, in turn, debates about those rights. These forces are changing our understanding of the world so quickly and profoundly that the task of reflecting upon them is as difficult for us as it is vital. The topic of divided cities offers one means of approaching the task. When and how does the diversity upon which cities thrive harden into division? What is being done and what more should be done in the struggle to remove urban divisions and to promote greater justice? Are the forces of globalization and migration proving a help or a hindrance? And what role can and should the concept of human rights play in the struggle?

This book proposes no straightforward answers to these questions. It offers instead a series of contrasting methodological and political perspectives upon them. Its contributors include leading theorists and practitioners—thinkers and doers alike—from a range of fields including urban studies and architecture, development economics, law, political theory, sociology, and psychoanalysis. The same contributors occupy different positions within an unusually wide spectrum of political perspectives and engagements: postmodern Marxists rub shoulders here with governmental advisers and international technocrats. The result of their collaboration is a book that brings together controversial and sometimes conflicting accounts of the topic and, in so doing, reflects the current troubled state of the urban debate. The book aims above all to inform and encourage readers who wish to think critically for themselves about the terms and implications of that debate. Its internal architecture—with the lectures each set in context by an individual introducer and then subjected as a whole to two overarching critical responses by experts in the field—is designed with that aim in mind.

As Stuart Hall observes in the first of the lectures, the character of cities has changed considerably in the last three decades. Hall, a groundbreaking sociologist of race and ethnicity, identifies globalization and mass migration as the two main reasons for this change. He considers whether, in this new context, the world will be able to ensure the cosmopolitan diversity of its cities without allowing them to split along potentially explosive lines of division. In so doing, he offers a complex panoramic account of the world's global cities, and one that opens up lines of enquiry pursued by other lecturers.

He points out, among other things, the specific danger posed to the cosmopolitan urban ideal by the attacks of 11 September 2001 and by the reaction in Western countries to '9/11' (as it is now commonly known); the increasing disparities in wealth and opportunity between the haves and the have-nots in the global economy; the visible signs of these disparities in urban landscapes and lifestyles; and the plight of the have-nots in the slums of the developing world and the homeless shelters of the developed world. Hall is largely pessimistic about the prospects for greater urban justice, equality, and diversity in the current 'neo-liberal' political climate and is keen to point out the gap between the cosmopolitan promises that globalization offers and the grim multicultural realities it has brought to the world's cities.

Patricia Williams pursues one of the lines of enquiry opened up by Hall in examining the so-called 'war on terror' declared by the American government in the wake of 9/11. A distinguished lawyer, she focuses on the effect that this 'war' is having on law and order in the cities of the United States, and points to a number of recent cases which reveal 'a tightening [of] the overlap between the tactics of outright war and the practices of urban policing'. She argues that such cases serve merely to reinforce existing social and racial divisions in American cities, about which she has written elsewhere, and to tip the balance too far away from enshrined ideals of due process, freedom, and rights towards the ever-increasing demands of national security. She is careful to acknowledge that she is describing a predominantly American trend, and one that is most clearly visible in New York City, for obvious reasons. But those who followed the case of the foreign terrorist suspects held contrary to the provisions of the European Convention on Human Rights and without trial at Belmarsh top security prison in south-east London may well feel that Williams's analysis is pertinent to current developments in the UK and in the other countries who have decided to join forces with the US in its 'war on terror'.[5] The question raised by Williams in her 2003 lecture, of what lengths governments should go to in the interests of national security, has undoubtedly taken on new urgency in the wake of the attacks that shook Madrid in March 2004 and London in July 2005.

David Harvey starts his lecture from a pessimistic analysis of globalization and its effect on cities worldwide similar to that offered by Stuart Hall. Unlike Hall, however, he goes on to espouse a radical utopian Marxist perspective from which he argues that cities can and should be reshaped by their citizens. If this is to happen, Harvey argues, then a revolution needs to take place in our conception of human rights. We live in a global capitalist society which rests upon fundamental rights of individual ownership and private property while considering other rights, such as the right to be treated with dignity, to be merely derivative. We need to overturn this hierarchy and recast the derivative individual right to dignity as a new fundamental collective right to the city, in other words, the right to 'make the city more in accord with our hearts' desire'. One practical consequence of this argument may be violent conflict in the city between those who hold equal but competing conceptions of human rights. Harvey acknowledges this in quoting Marx's dictum, 'between such equal rights only force can decide', and suggests that the city has long been and remains the key locus of such conflicts. The right to the city which he passionately advocates has, for this very reason, 'to be seized by political movement' from below.

David Harvey and James Wolfensohn share a basic commitment to the promotion of equity or fairness for all. They share little else in political terms, however, and their lectures, which sit side by side in the middle of this volume, offer diametrically opposed analyses of how equity is to be achieved in the world's cities. For Harvey, a Marxist urban theorist, globalization reinforces social and economic inequity; for Wolfensohn, President of the World Bank at the time of his Oxford Amnesty Lecture and a pragmatist who talks in terms of rational self-interest more readily than he does in terms of rights, the opposite is true: globalization promotes greater equity by forcing the international community to recognize its common political and economic interest in fighting poverty wherever it is found. Wolfensohn shares the stated view of the UN Secretary-General, Kofi Annan, that 'the locus of global poverty is moving to the cities', those of the developing world in particular.[6] He argues that the most effective way of fighting poverty in the slums of the developing world is to use international aid and private investment to create the conditions in which slum residents can work for and invest in the betterment of their own communities. Slum residents need to enjoy the same social recognition as their neighbours and the same access to secure housing, education, and healthcare. The cities in which they live need to be governed by healthy political, economic, and legal and judicial institutions if they are to attract external investment. The new development paradigm, which operates on these principles, successfully harnesses the resources available from above and below, Wolfensohn argues, citing as his main example the World Bank's ongoing Cities Without Slums action plan. This plan, he claims, is helping to make the divided cities of the developing world a thing of the past.

The challenge of building undivided cities is by no means confined to the developing world. As Richard Rogers observes in his lecture, England is already the most densely populated country in the world after Bangladesh and Holland, and in the next twenty years it needs to accommodate 4 million more households. How best can this need be met? An architect of international renown, Rogers is also the Labour peer who chaired the government-commissioned Urban Task Force Report on British cities, 'Towards an Urban Renaissance' (1999). Very few of the recommendations in that report have so far been implemented, as Rogers makes clear in his lecture before criticizing this as a failure of the Labour government that he has served. In renewing his call for an urban Renaissance in twenty-first-century Britain, Rogers argues that its cities should be more densely populated, ecologically sustainable, equitable, and—last but not least—more beautiful. He emphasizes the connections between the built and social environments of cities: physical dereliction reflects and promotes social exclusion as much as beautiful buildings do civic pride. If an urban Renaissance is both possible and desirable, it is because, in Rogers's view, 'people make cities, and cities make citizens'.

For all their differences of conviction and approach, Rogers, Wolfensohn, and Harvey all assume that the most destitute people in cities share with other human beings the capacity to be motivated by the will to self-betterment and by a sense of responsibility. In the last of the lectures, a study of the long-term homeless of Paris, Patrick Declerck challenges this fundamental assumption along with the concepts of social 'exclusion' and 'inclusion' it supports. A psychoanalyst with the philosopher's talent for dissecting the ideas that most of us hold dear, Declerck has practical experience of his subject, since he spent years working with the homeless of Paris and observing their lives at close quarters. His lecture offers a close description of what it is to be down and out on the streets of a big city and a psychoanalytic explanation of why it is that some people remain in this position year after year. Both make uncomfortable reading. Declerck argues that, in staying on the streets, the long-term homeless exhibit a symptom of the extreme masochism that determines the course of their lives; and that, in keeping them on the streets, mainstream society reveals a sadistic desire visibly to punish those who do not accept the obligations of social existence. The sado-masochist relationship that exists between those who live on the streets and the mainstream society of the so-called 'developed' world explains why, for both groups, the suffering of the homeless is 'necessary'.

Each of the six lectures in this book can be read as an independent piece in its own right. But significant points of convergence and conflict also emerge between them, as this introduction has suggested, and the last section of the book is designed to develop these points further and to offer a critical overview of the ground covered. That this section should consist of two conflicting responses to the lectures, as it does, seems entirely appropriate. The two respondents, Michael Likosky and Peter Hall, both focus on the rela-tionship between political and economic globalization and urban poverty. Likosky, a specialist in international economic law, sides with Stuart Hall and David Harvey against James Wolfensohn in insisting that globalization only increases the divide between the wealthy few and the impoverished many in the world's cities. He argues that the new development paradigm being adopted by the World Bank and its partners effectively forces the urban poor to pay for what should be their birthright, namely, the basic infrastructure of the city in which they live. Peter Hall, an urban historian and

Professor of Planning who has worked as an adviser to the UK government, takes the opposite view and insists that 'overwhelming' empirical evidence supports Wolfensohn's case that the new development paradigm works. Hall adopts a polemical tone in his response, accusing the critics of globalization and urbanization in the volume of taking a 'delight in doomery and gloomery'. By ending as it does in this way, the volume acquires a precarious balance of its own, since it began with the other (and unrelated) Hall sending polemical shafts in the opposite direction and dismissing talk of a 'new win-win global economy' as 'manifestly utopian nonsense'. Seen from this perspective, the book appears to be a tale of two Halls, poised uneasily—as cities have long been in the imagination—between visions of utopia and dystopia.

The aim of this book is not to decide for its readers which of the two Halls, Stuart or Peter, is closer to the truth. Its aim, as has already been made clear, is to allow readers to explore and examine the various arguments for themselves. It is not a 'campaigning' book, or rather, its sole campaign is for the provocation of more and better thinking about the topic in question. Montaigne, the sixteenth-century French humanist mentioned earlier, is famous for having revived and popularized the ancient sceptical practice of perpetually seeking the truth in all matters of opinion by weighing, as if in a pair of scales, each proposition against its opposite. Montaigne's pair of scales offers an accurate image for this book. How to achieve greater justice in the world's cities is a question to whose complexities no single volume of essays, even one as diverse as this, can do full justice. This book can and does, however, aim to offer its readers, as the 2003 Oxford Amnesty Lectures did their audiences, a broad range of the relevant arguments and the means to weigh them against one another.

Offering such a range of arguments has been possible only thanks to the willingness of all the contributors to participate in the debate. Participation required the lecturers to set out their views to a large public audience in Oxford University's Sheldonian Theatre, to answer questions from the floor after their lecture, and to agree to publish revised versions of their lectures in this volume. The decision of the Oxford Amnesty Lectures committee to invite James Wolfensohn to participate in its 2003 series sparked controversy in the streets of Oxford and inside the Sheldonian Theatre. Wolfensohn's lecture on 19 February 2003 was heckled and at times drowned out by demonstrators who saw it as unacceptable that the President of the World Bank should be speaking in front of an Amnesty International banner. These protests led Oxford Amnesty Lectures, not to reconsider its invitation to Wolfensohn, but to restate, on its website and in the press, its identity and purposes. Oxford Amnesty Lectures is not part of Amnesty International. It is an independent charity created to sustain debate about human rights in the academic and wider community and, in so doing, to raise funds for Amnesty International. Wolfensohn's lecture proved particularly successful on both counts. It attracted a huge paying audience, eager to hear what Wolfensohn had to say and to ask him questions, and it took place in circumstances that provoked debate, not just about the aspirations and the work of the World Bank in cities all over the developing world, but also about the right to freedom of expression in Oxford itself. In its pursuit of its aims and purposes, Oxford Amnesty Lectures will continue to exercise its right to invite speakers who may prove controversial. Lectures that take place in the absence of demonstrations make for an altogether more comfortable experience. Freedom of expression, however, rarely provides the comforts of unanimity.

Part I
Lectures

Introduction to Stuart Hall

Stephen Howe

Stuart Hall has inspired, influenced, and often provoked at least two generations of scholars and activists, across Britain and far beyond. He has held distinguished academic positions in both Cultural Studies (a discipline, or discourse, in whose making and remaking he has been a central figure) and Sociology. But his ideas and their impact have not been, and could not be, confined to any disciplinary mould, nor to the academic world alone. He has written on and been a significant and original voice in debates on popular culture, media and the arts, Thatcherism and the future of the Left, Marx and Gramsci, modernism and postmodernism, racial theories and race relations, concepts of diaspora, globalization, ethnicity, identity, and hybridity—and even that is just a near-random selection from among the themes that his work has addressed. His influence may be encountered, his name invoked, among artists and film-makers, especially younger black British ones, as well as academics. Strikingly, in a recent poll seeking to rank the '100 Greatest Black Britons', Hall was the only living intellectual to feature at all prominently (at no. 10) among musicians, sportspeople, and TV personalities. This polymathic presence does not, however, extend to absolute ubiquity: it should be pointed out that the presenter of the once-popular TV show 'It's a Knockout' was an entirely different Stuart Hall.

Our Stuart Hall is, on the face of it, very much a 'public intellectual'. This is a label more familiar in America than in

Britain, and one which sometimes seems to mean 'glib, media-friendly polemicist'. That is clearly not Hall at all, and perhaps the idea of the public intellectual fits him better if it is redefined: not (just) as someone who appears frequently in the public sphere, but as one whose efforts have always been directed towards defending and extending that sphere, its integrity, democracy, and inclusiveness. It is an ethical as well as a political endeavour. Hall's lifelong adherence to it, no less than the subject-matter and intellectual power of his essay here, makes him an apt choice to open this collection of Oxford Amnesty Lectures.

Hall was born in Kingston, Jamaica in 1932. He came to England, and to Oxford, as a Rhodes Scholar in 1951. He has recalled how his intensely Anglophile, conservative, and status-conscious mother 'delivered me, signed and sealed, to where she thought a son of hers had always belonged— Oxford'.[1] She worried, he says, that he might be 'mistaken for one of those immigrants'; but a few years later, learning that he had become prominently involved in left-wing political activism, she urged: 'Stay over there, don't come back here and make trouble for us with those funny ideas.'

To the great good fortune of Britain's intellectual and cultural life, Hall did stay over here and become one of those immigrants. It took some time, he says, before he decided to do so. His early years in Britain were 'saturated in West Indian expatriate politics', and he was intensely involved too in the wider anti-colonialist campaigning of the era. That connection was never broken: Hall's engagement with political, intellectual, and cultural developments in the Caribbean, as well as among its diasporas in Britain and elsewhere, remained close. Indeed, such themes have had a renewed salience in his writing since the 1990s, often now seasoned with autobiographical reflection. But his activities and earlier writings were far from confined to this. He was a prime mover in what has been called the British 'First New Left' of the 1950s. He was a founder and editor of *Universities and Left Review* with Charles Taylor, Gabriel Pearson, and the late Raphael Samuel, then the first editor of *New Left Review*, over whose sometimes stormy progress he presided until 1961. Meanwhile he taught, first in London schools as a supply teacher, then at Chelsea College where he lectured on media, film, and popular culture. His first book, co-written with Paddy Whannel and a pioneering investigation of those fields, was *The Popular Arts* (1964).

Many of Hall's subsequent books have also been co-authored or co-edited with friends and colleagues, reflecting the emphasis he has always placed on intellectual work as a cooperative endeavour, on thinking together with others. These include *Policing the Crisis* (1978), *Culture, Media, Language* (1980), and *The Idea of the Modern State* (1984). The *Hard Road to Renewal* (1988), his collected writings on the impact of Margaret Thatcher, were widely hailed as among the most insightful, in some cases even prophetic, analyses of modern British Conservatism. He is sometimes credited, or blamed, with inventing the very term 'Thatcherism', but has disclaimed this dubious honour.

From 1972 to 1979, Hall was Director of the Centre for Contemporary Cultural Studies at Birmingham University. This was a remarkable institution, and a remarkable period. The CCCS, in its initial incarnation under Richard Hoggart, had been the originating focal point for the serious study of popular culture, not only in Britain but worldwide. Under Hall's directorship, staff and students there not only continued to make groundbreaking contributions to this field—with his own still to the fore—but diversified astonishingly into pioneering work on Marxist theory, ideology, the politics of gender, race, and empire, public history, and more. One suitable response to those who noisily doubt the intellectual value and rigour of academic cultural studies, who think it amounts to no more than 'The Semiotics of Beer-mats' or 'Why Madonna's Better than Mozart', would be to point to the often abstruse, demanding, and intensely theoretical writings that Hall and others produced from Birmingham in those years.

At the Open University, where Hall was Professor of Sociology until his retirement in 1997, he brought his extraordinary energy, intellectual range and critical skills to yet wider audiences through the TV and radio series which the OU made for its 'long-distance learning' adult student body. To refer to Hall's 'retirement' is quite misleading, for the subsequent years have seen no diminution in his flow of writing and other work. Yet despite all the books, all the articles, broadcasts, and edited collections, all the activity as inspiring teacher, editor, and energizer of others' undertakings, Hall's greatest gifts (in both senses: the qualities he has, and what he gives to others) may be as an essayist and a lecturer. He is insistent on the value of the 'intervention': a piece of writing or public speaking that is very much of its moment, that seeks to make a difference to a particular argument in a specific time and place, but also to go beyond that and say something wider and of more lasting significance. The essay or public lecture is ideally suited to such interventions, and Hall has long been a master or the art.

The text that follows is a marvellous instance. He views the contemporary city—global, multicultural, so full of promise and possibility yet also so disjointed, unequal, and dangerous—as a product of two massive, interdependent forces:

globalization and mass migration. It is by no means entirely new: Hall, unlike many of those who work in similar scholarly fields, has always been alert to the demands of history and emphasizes that novel patterns are 'grafted on to well-established historical forms of the city'. But original social and spatial divisions are now emerging, and with them unfamiliar challenges to our understanding, to our competence in political or social action, and to our ethical sense.

What he is doing here is, arguably, what almost all his work since the 1950s has attempted: to trace connections between particular current social trends and broad theoretical models that seek to explain them. This, for him, involves always a double movement: on the one hand, asking how specific phenomena can be illuminated by theory, and on the other, trying to put the theoretical conceptions to immediate, practical, politically and morally engaged *use*. Attempting to explain complex changes in both urban social (and spatial) *structures* and in social *identities*, in their ever-shifting relationship to one another, what he says is informed by a theoretical consciousness both intense and wide-ranging—critics would say, eclectic. But it deliberately refuses to propose a general theoretical model abstracted from distinct contexts and uses. This can make Hall's mode of argument frustrating for those who want clear-cut, generalizable formulae, just as his equally characteristic insistence on both positive and negative aspects of present trends resolutely frustrates those who want a singular and simple political 'lesson'. The sheer range, the deftness of synthesis, the boldness of insight are striking. But perhaps even more so is Stuart Hall's finely balanced alertness both to old and to new, to tradition and innovation, his continued capacity (in his own words) to 'honour the moment you're trying to transcend'.

Cosmopolitan Promises, Multicultural Realities

Stuart Hall

These reflections take as their focus the contemporary 'global/multicultural' city, which has emerged in recent years as a new type of urban configuration. They are written largely in reference to the UK and, more particularly though not exclusively, to London. The global/multicultural pattern is not absolutely novel: it has been grafted on to well-established historical forms of the city. However, the social and spatial configurations of London and other metropolitan cities have been significantly reshaped or 'translated' in recent years by many forces, two of which—globalization and migration—are foregrounded here. In the course of my argument, I will expand on why the two terms 'global' and 'multicultural', which often seem to point in different directions and to different realities, are so closely juxtaposed in my account; and I will discuss the relationship between the processes of globalization and migration that underpin them. My particular concern is with the new social and spatial divisions in the city which are emerging as a consequence of the interdependence between new forms of globalization and new patterns of migration, and the distinctive tensions and conflicts to which they give rise.

Cities are the product—the material and spatial expression—of their times. In the nineteenth and twentieth centuries, the great English cities were motors of industrial production and centres of world trade, commerce, and finance. Some were also integrated into the networks of imperial power and colonial trade as monuments to the imperial life of the nation. Later, cities became the sites for a modernist aesthetics of corporate power, a development more evident in New York and elsewhere in the US, as the axis of world power shifted westwards, than in Europe. Western cities are no longer like this, though their transformations are slow, complicated, and highly uneven.

Many forces have been at work in bringing about change, but I draw attention here to three. The first is the uneven transition from an industrial to a post-industrial economy and society. Cities today not only embody this shift towards the service and information economy, but vividly represent the dislocations which have inevitably accompanied this process of de-industrialization. The second is globalization. Of course, globalization has taken many forms in history. A kind of globalization has been in progress since Europe broke out of its confines towards the end of the fifteenth century, and began to construct the beginnings of a world market and to explore, conquer, subdue by trade and naval power, and ultimately to colonize much of the rest of the globe. But the globalization I have in mind here is that represented by the new forms of the 'global' economy, based on the multinational capitalist corporation and augmented financial flows, which began to emerge in the mid-1970s. The third factor is migration. Migration is often understood as subsidiary to—a mere unintended consequence of—a more general 'globalization' process. However, I want to explore more fully the intricate, but also disjunctive, relations between the new forms of globalization and the new patterns of migration. What concerns me especially is how the ethnic, social, and cultural diversity that results necessarily from migration is changing the face of the modern urban landscape and reconfiguring the social divisions and conflicts characteristic of so-called 'global' cities.

The worldwide movement of peoples across the globe is, in its scale, composition, direction, and diversity, a phenomenon of world significance. There are more people 'on the move' across the globe than at any time in modern history —whether driven by persistent poverty, underdevelopment, hunger, and unemployment, by the modern pandemics of disease and ill-heath, ecological devastation, and environmental disaster, or by civil war, ethnic cleansing, religious or tribal conflict. The cities of the developed world exercise a magnetic pull over this human tide, thereby reversing the historic flows associated with the imperial cities of recent centuries. We need to understand better than we do the far-reaching consequences of this global movement, its connection with emerging configurations of economic and geopolitical power, the new patterns of conflict it sets in play, and their implications for the wider pursuit of equality and social justice.

The great African-American civil rights leader, W. E. B. Dubois, once prophesied that the key problem of the twentieth century would be 'the problem of the colour line'. Events in recent years have led one to wonder whether, looking back with hindsight at the twenty-first century, historians may not be tempted to say that its problem was the much-denied but manifest 'clash of civilizations', in which 'the colour line' continues to play a significant (though transformed) role, and of which world migration is one major symptom. One question that the 'clash of civilizations' raises is what I have called elsewhere 'the multicultural question'.[1] This arises with particular salience when the 'clash' occurs within the metropolises of the developed world.

The multicultural question runs something like this: What are the chances that we can construct in our cities shared, diverse, just, more inclusive, and egalitarian forms of common life, guaranteeing the full rights of democratic citizenship and participation to all on the basis of equality, whilst respecting the differences that inevitably come about when peoples of different religions, cultures, histories, languages, and traditions are obliged to live together in the same shared space? Can they do so without falling apart—socially, spatially, politically— into warring and embattled enclaves, or, alternatively, without those in power engaging in punitive 'missionary' campaigns to obliterate difference and make everyone become more like them? How can shared, reciprocal forms of life emerge, given the glaring disparities of power, recognition, and material and symbolic resources between the different elements?

These issues have to be addressed both in terms of what cities are or are becoming, and of how they are imagined and represented. Though these two facets relate to different domains of practice, I do not propose to make any sharp distinction between them. Like Benedict Anderson's 'imagined communities', cities are always both socially, economically, and culturally constituted and, at the same time, configured in the imaginary through the regimes of representation. That cities are also spatially constituted, and that disposition in and across space is both a fact of social organization (the urban economy) and a regime of representation (architecture and planning), make cities a critical zone of mediation between these two aspects. It goes without saying that how cities are imagined has real effects upon how they are lived, and vice versa. Their spatial character gives the city a particular visible intelligibility, allowing it to be 'read'. Indeed, the city itself may be conceived in some respects as a 'machinery of representation', because of its nearly unique role in materializing social relationships in space. It sets in motion a complex reciprocity in the sphere of the urban between 'being' and 'seeing', living and looking, of which Baudelaire and Walter Benjamin, theorists of the *flâneur*, were conceptual pioneers.

Cities have always been divided. They are divided by class and wealth, by rights to and over property, by occupation and use, by lifestyle and culture, by race and nationality, ethnicity and religion, and by gender and sexuality. The template of these social divisions can be read into the differentiated zones of the city's cartography. The well-off and the rich, the propertied and the corporate, the entrepreneurial and the middle classes, the professionals and the clericals, the artisans and the poor, the underclasses and the outcast, have always occupied different areas of the city. The boundaries between these spaces, however, have never been entrenched. They merge and overlap at their invisible borders, shift and change across time. Often, boundaries are more informally than formally marked and maintained. The various zones, however distinctive to those who know how to 'read' on the run, are never uniform in look or homogeneous in social composition. Differences edge, slide, and blur into one another. They overlay one another, creating a complex, overlapping matrix or palimpsest effect. These juxtapositions and overlaps may be multiplying: this is one of the dimensions along which the contemporary city is said to be changing most quickly. However, intangible as these boundaries often are and maintained as they are by complex cultural and social codes legible only to those who practise them on a daily basis in the banal routines of everyday life, they tend nevertheless to divide the city into distinct, though not tightly bounded or impenetrable, clusters.

On the other hand, cities also bring elements together and establish relations of interchange and exchange between them. They connect different life-worlds and temporalities, the space-time combinations that Bakhtin calls 'chronotopes'. They function as spatial magnets for different, converging streams of human activity. That is why cities have a very long history as centres of trade, as markets, and thus as sites of cultural exchange and social complexity. This is the basis of their often unplanned 'cosmopolitanism'. The points of convergence, as well as the routes and passages through and across them, are as significant as the spatially defined and socially maintained differences. Cities both divide and connect. They condense difference. Inevitably, they are caught in a double rhythm of involvement and exclusion, proximity and separation, fixity and fluidity.

This aspect has been considerably intensified—but also modified—in the new 'global' conditions. The question for us is how these complex impulses of homogeneity and diversity are working out and how the cartography of the contemporary city is being gradually reconfigured under the impact of globalization and migration. Here the metaphor of the palimpsest is particularly apposite: one layer is to be seen superimposed on another, in which the lines of definition of an older pattern persist and continue to invade the surface even as another, more recent patina overlays it. In significant ways, the old, hierarchical ordering of urban space seems to have disappeared for good.[2] As Bridge and Watson put it:

Global cities are a result of transactions that fragment space, such that we can no longer talk about global cities as whole cities— instead, what we have [are] bits of cities that are highly globalized— and bits juxtaposed that are completely cut out [from the globalizing process] [. . .] In this sense, some parts of cities can have more in common with parts of other global cities or cities in the same region than with the part of the city [most closely] juxtaposed. This valorization and devalorization of space goes hand in hand, and in many places is becoming more and more extreme.

Urban centres nevertheless concentrate enormous power and potential global control [. . .] The devalued sectors which rest largely on the labour of women [and] immigrants [. . .] represent a terrain where battles are fought on many fronts and in many sites and these battles lack clear boundaries.[3]

Some of the forces driving these changes are undoubtedly related to the new forms of globalization that emerged in the mid-1970s. They reflect the new division of labour to have occurred as a result of the general decline of manufacturing in the developed West and its transnationalization to other, less developed parts of the globe, with which corporate and financial centres in the West can remain connected through 'space-time condensations' which the new technologies of finance and communication make possible.[4] This is a division of labour more appropriate to the new service- and information-led economy. These forces for change are associated with the dominance of the transnational corporation, the renewed power of finance capital, the pace of global investment flows, currency switching, and the spread of a global consumer culture and media disseminating, largely from the West, images of 'the Good Life'. These are the engines of the now hegemonic deregulating, free-market, privatizing, neo-liberal economic regime known appropriately in another context as 'the Washington Consensus' and to which, incidentally, New Labour in the UK is a paid-up, loyal, junior signatory. These forces constitute and define the true, substantial meaning and content of that deceptive term 'the global'.

They, in turn, have been integrated within a planetary strategy designed to open up the world, especially the developing 'South', to the twin gods of the neo-liberal revolution —free markets and liberal democracy—which, in Fukuyama's terms, have brought all history to an end within a single planetary system or world order.[5] This is now the governing world system, rooted economically in the free play of deregulated market forces, global capitalist penetration, the privatization of public goods, the monopoly of scarce or valuable resources, the dismantling of welfare and health programmes, and the lure of 'free trade' between profoundly unequal partners on a fundamentally skewed playing field.

The decolonization that occurred at the end of World War II, often hailed as 'setting the colonial world free', was in fact marked by three broad stages redefining relations between the developed West and the rest. In the first phase, fundamental relations of neocolonial dependency were established between the developed and underdeveloped worlds in the context of the Cold War. In this phase, the difficult problems of establishing independent post-colonial states on the basis of autonomous economies were redefined as and subordinated to the struggle between the two rival camps: the Cold War was fought out largely by proxy on post-colonial terrain. In the second phase, 'structural adjustment' regimes were imposed by the West on the developing world, via international organizations coupled with massive indebtedness through the banking system. More recently, with the collapse of the Soviet empire and the rise of the US to single superpower hegemony, an unholy alliance of global corporate forces, collusive indigenous elites, and legal and illegal armies on the loose has been able to treat the world's poor and the societies of the South as open marketplaces, repositories of

27

scarce resources, and reservoirs of cheap labour. These are open to those corporate global agents best positioned to exploit them under the canopy of a form of 'global governance' provided by international agencies such as the IMF, the World Bank, and the WTO, whose disasters are mopped up by UN humanitarian, NGO, charitable, and foreign aid programmes.

If earlier phases of globalization worked through conquest, trade, mercantile and naval supremacy, direct colonization, imperial investment, and mandated rule—all of which left their indelible imprint on the cities of the metropole in former times—the new system operates through a double repertoire: routinely, 'at a distance', through market forces and geopolitical and global economic management; but also, at moments of crisis, through strategic military intervention in distant places. One of the principal unintended consequences of this 'new world order', though it is in no sense reducible to an economic logic, has been to secure the conditions for the 'free' reproduction of global inequalities. The world has, of course, been riveted by the military, strategic, and geopolitical consequences of these processes, especially in terms of the US-led role in the Middle East, the oil-rich Gulf states, Afghanistan, and Iraq. The role of covert US-inspired intervention—which has been a constant feature of the geopolitical system since the end of World War II—has, in the new situation of single-power dominance, become a matter of overt and systematic strategy based on overwhelming military and economic power. The civilian disaster of September 11, 2001 no doubt concentrated minds and hardened hearts, and the 'war' on a generalized Terror has drawn many states—some of them reluctantly—into the orbit of a new 'humanitarian interventionism'. But few have tried to

connect the hatreds and resentments which drive the fundamentalist assault on Western power and values with the massive planetary imbalances in life chances between the world's
rich and marginalized poor which are driven by the new
neo-liberal 'world system'.

Hardt and Negri, in the widely-discussed volume which
names the emerging new world order as an imperial one,
argue that the 'informal networks of Empire' are no longer
directly related to the power of nation-states.[6] This has a certain validity: the new system is essentially transnational. But in
the interests of underlining the radical novelty of the present,
and too eager to underline the self-sustaining and systemic
character of globalization, the authors overplay this aspect
in describing it as 'a system without a centre'. In the radical
terms in which they advance the argument, this claim is
both true and not true. Even in a transnational system, large
Western nation-states remain key players, though more and
more often as partners in larger regional groupings or 'coalitions'. It is also true that they are able to operate less and less
independently of the global system which sustains them,
because their role in this system is the stake on which their
power increasingly depends. In the developing world, it could
be said that it is the failure to establish strong, independent
nation-states that has been the problem, and that where such
states have been successful—as, for example, in South-East
Asia—strong states and independent national state policies
have been the secret of their success.

The post-9/11 situation suggests, on the contrary, that the
so-called new world order is one in which the US, the only
remaining super-power, has an overwhelming influence. It
does so less as an old-style colonizing nation—at which, if the
disaster that is Iraq currently is any measure, it is hopelessly

incompetent—and more as a global nation-state: the nodal power-centre of a wide-ranging global, geopolitical, economic, military, and strategic network which is nevertheless deeply imprinted with American cultural values and national interests. The US is thus an exceptional case: it is a rich and powerful nation state and also the leading 'market state',[7] with a massive internal market, productive economy, advanced technology, land, and raw materials; but it is also a state whose planetary power nevertheless depends on its transnational character and global economic, cultural, geopolitical, and military reach. This is the nature of the 'new imperialism' which is reshaping the globe.

All this has consequences for global/multicultural cities, which are linked to this new world-system of power through corporate global economic networks, rather than in their earlier function as the city bases of giant industrial firms, as centres of imperial investment, national greatness, and colonial rule. Their characteristic new skyline is now increasingly dominated by the corporate headquarters of globally dispersed transnational companies, surrounded by their ancillary and supportive out-sourced dependencies in financial services, marketing, banking, investment, advertising, design, and information technologies. The urban architecture which mirrors this shift is most paradigmatically to be found in Canary Wharf-style corporate 'towers' of glass and steel, functionally exposed transparent cubes or architect-inspired cucumber-shaped pods now dominating financial centres and urban skylines around the globe: the corporate 'canyons' of the City of London around Bishopsgate and Liverpool Street rather than the porticoed splendour of the Natural History and Science Museums, the Victoria and Albert, Imperial College, and Royal Albert Hall, those monuments to Victorian and

Edwardian imperial grandeur, with their South Kensington satellite of trendy streets, neo-Georgian town-houses and the great department-store shopping emporia.

Since the mid-1970s, the forces we have been identifying have, with rapidly increasing intensity, intervened across the world to influence the strategies and steer the social, political, and economic outcomes of 'development' in a neo-liberal, free-market, deregulative, open-investment, free-trade, 'trickle-down' direction. They have radically rewritten the domestic political agenda of former developed welfare states, bringing to an end the historic compromise between capital and labour that defined the social-democratic character of the immediate post-war settlement, and driving these societies towards what Philip Bobbitt calls the 'market-state model' and all major political parties and governments towards the centre-right ground of what has been called a 'one-party politics'. These are the lines of force that bind together the domestic and international political agendas of 'caring' neo-conservatism in the US and New Labour's hybrid version of modernizing Third Way neo-liberalism.[8] They connect the so-called 'reform agenda' in the UK domestically with the new doctrine of 'humanitarian interventionism' and pre-emptive strike in the geopolitical and strategic arena. This new world order must be made safe globally for liberal democracy and the free market economy—defended where necessary by 'shock and awe', or 'measured force', as Mao Tse Tung and President George W. Bush would, in their different ways, put it.

Meanwhile, the promises designed to make the poor complicit with their global fate—rising living standards, a more equal distribution of goods and life chances, an opportunity to compete on equal terms with the developed world, a fairer share of the world's wealth—have comprehensively failed to be delivered. Both the trickle-down theory of wealth redistribution and the manifestly utopian nonsense about a 'new win-win global economy' have proved themselves to be the waste material of yesterday's common sense so far as large sections of the 'developing' world are concerned. The product of the upswing in the economic cycle has vanished into thin air as the cycle turns down and the war-clouds gather. Those at home and their allies in the new states who profited from the massive inflation in shareholder value largely escaped the downturn unscathed, although a few, such as Enron, were caught out before they could find cover.

The poor of the world, however, did not escape. The gaping difference in the distribution of economic, social, cultural resources across the world has remorselessly widened. The UN-Habitat Report, commenting on the unprecedented rising rate of urbanization, recently reported that the global urban population increased by 36 per cent in the 1990s and that there are 550 million urban slum dwellers in Asia, 187 million in Africa, and 128 million in Latin America and the Caribbean. The new megalopolises of the developing world, with their New York-style financial city centres floating like glittering glass islands in a veritable ocean of poverty-stricken and drug-ridden *favelas*, are the urban markers of this process. Even the thirty richest countries in the world account for another 54 million urban poor. Globalization, *The Guardian* reported on 10 October 2003,

has partly caused and greatly exacerbated the perilous social and physical condition of slum dwellers [. . .] The new insecurities that globalization has caused are legion, with barely any benefits going to the poor [. . .] Dominant 'neo-liberal' economic doctrines [. . .] have explicitly demanded an increase in inequality, including the reduction of all government welfare spending, the privatization of everything that the state controlled, the reform of regulation and the removal of planning restrictions.

The rapidly growing disparities between the haves and the have-nots, which is glaringly obvious at the global level, are being reproduced within the richest societies of the developed world. Following the long period of levelling incomes and wealth after World War II—the era of redistributive welfare states—these inequalities began to rise exponentially after 1980. The gap between rich and poor in the UK is wider now than when New Labour took power in 1997. The richest 1 per cent of Americans own more than 40 per cent of the nation's wealth. Even in the UK, the comparable figure is as much as 18 per cent, and the top 20 per cent are richer than the bottom 29 per cent by a ratio of 9.6 to 1; in the US, it is by a ratio of 11 to 1.[9] Meanwhile, millions in the US are still without any form of health insurance and more than 3 million children remain below current restrictive definitions of the poverty line in Britain, even in a period when child poverty has been one of the areas targeted for reform.

At the same time, the powers seeking to impose permanently adverse terms of trade on the poor countries of the South through free-trade open investment regimes, and defending the right of transnational corporations (energy, pharmaceutical, biotechnology, and agribusiness interests especially) to buy up basic public utilities, patent the genetic sequences of natural products, subsidize and dump cheap commodities, drive out indigenous producers, and pay day-labourers below subsistence wages, have come together to design a new World Trade Organization round, which the vigorous but belated opposition of some developing societies only temporarily delayed at the Cancun WTO meeting in 2003. No Western economy has been known successfully to develop, with benefits for the majority of its population, under the conditions such a regime would impose. The delay, however, is only temporary. The major economic powers are determined to return to this privatizing free-trade agenda.

Reliance on market forces as the sole driver of global economic and social development has brought in its train other insuperable problems that have an indirect impact on social life: ecological and environmental disaster, the disruption of the fragile balance of indigenous economies, disease epidemics, the massive exploitation of rural low-wage labour, the destruction of peasant farming and of subsistence agriculture, and the collapse of world commodity prices. The result has been rapid and unsustainable urbanization and—coupled with collapsing post-colonial state regimes, civil unrest, and the militarization of ethnic conflict—the phenomenon of mass migration. These global disasters form the invisible infrastructure of the changing cartography of globalization/ migration and are powerful contributors to the only too visible crisis of the metropolitan city.

Migration is increasingly the joker in the globalization pack, the subterranean circuit connecting the crisis of one part of the global system with the growth rates and living standards of the other. The logic of globalization says that every element of growth must be free to move fluidly across every regulative boundary, including that of the nation-state: capital, investment, commodities, technologies, currencies, profits, cultural messages, and images all flow. Ideologically, barriers must be thrown over, the circuits kept open. In fact, the reality is something different: all the major proponents of free trade and open investment borders manage, in practice, to impose their own selective preferential regimes where it is in their national interest to do so. However, when the model is working perfectly, only one commodity—labour—is required to stay still or to be strictly controlled in its movement. Otherwise, how can transnational corporations take 'competitive advantage' of the cheap labour, low wage conditions, tax breaks, and favourable investment regimes offered by developing societies? Suppose thousands of workers in Bangladesh, Indonesia, the Republic of the Congo, or Guatemala were free to desert their one-dollar-a-day jobs and turn up as high-waged labour in the high-tech economies of the cities of the American west coast? The fact that, in the UK, small numbers of highly trained and scarce workers (such as computer technicians and nurses) and untrained, unemployed seasonal labourers willing to work in shocking conditions at below minimum wage levels (such as fruit-pickers, kitchen porters, and building labourers) are encouraged to migrate in selective and controlled numbers—in keeping with the uncertain rhythms of the labour market—does not undermine the general model.

Nevertheless, and in spite of the logic of the system, there has been an unprecedented explosion in the largely unplanned movement of peoples across the globe. Whether fleeing the consequences of mass poverty, malnutrition, and unemployment in search of better economic or personal opportunities, or displaced by political violence, regime change, persecution, religious conflict, ethnic cleansing, or civil war, those people stigmatized as 'economic migrants', refugees, and asylum-seekers now constitute the homeless multitudes of the modern metropolitan city. Seeking by whatever means—legal or illegal—to escape the consequences of globalization and the new world order, they move along uncharted routes, secrete themselves in the most inhospitable interstices, mortgage their worldly goods to the human traffickers, seal life-threatening contracts with gang-masters and pimps, and exploit their lateral family connections in order to subvert the physical barriers, legal constraints, and immigration regimes that metropolitan powers are vigorously putting in place. These are the overspill of the global system, the world's surplus populations, the *sans-papiers* of the modern metropolis, who slip across borders at the dead of night or stow away in the backs of lorries or under trains and silently disappear into the hidden depths of the city. This is the human face of the new globalization 'from below'. The global cities of the developed world are the sluice-gates of this new tidal movement.

In earlier phases, the problems of religious, social, and cultural difference were largely kept at a safe distance from the metropolitan homelands of imperial systems. Metropolitan liberals, long distanced from the day-to-day management of slave and plantation regimes or mining outposts in the tropics, could indulge themselves with the thought that, when finally the full benefits of the slave trade had been extracted, Britain had vigorously pursued the ships on the high seas still engaged in that nefarious traffic. On this slippery foundation a great deal of national self-congratulation has been constructed. Today, the new kinds of differences whose deep, underlying causes we have sketched, intrude directly into the heart of the Western metropolitan city, disturb, challenge, and undermine the social and political space of its urban centres, disrupt its long-settled class equilibrium, and subvert its relatively homogenous cultural character. They challenge the idea that the nation-state is the sole source and effective guardian of human rights or a universally democratic conception of citizenship. They project the vexed issue of global poverty, social and religious pluralism, and cultural difference into the largely settled monocultural spaces of the Western metropolis. This produces an epistemic rupture and a new social problematic —that of the post-colonial paradigm.

The global city has been significantly transformed by these forces. They have had massive effects upon the spatial, social, and cultural reconfiguring of cities, as the old industrial city's material ecology declines and social strata whose interrelationships were forged in the crucible of industrialization, mass production, democratization, and imperial hegemony change in orientation, composition, and lifestyle. Manufacturing in Britain is now in general decline, and large-scale industrial production no longer dominates city centres, governs their economies, or defines the character and tempo of their social life as they once did. These are now often urban areas of extensive social deprivation and economic dislocation, endemic unemployment, and environmental degradation as well as sites of a widespread social despair and hopelessness leading to the defensive mobilization of difference—and thus of ethnic tension, intra-class hostility, racial conflict, social alienation, and civil unrest.

In the wake of civil disturbances between white residents and Muslim youths in northern British industrial towns and cities such as Bradford, Oldham, and Burnley in 2001, Kundani observed that in such places in earlier times, 'the textile industry was the common thread binding the White and Asian working class into a single social fabric. But with its collapse, each community was forced to turn inwards on to itself.'[10] This has been compounded by the long drift towards ethnic segregation in neighbourhood housing and in schools, a breakdown in communication between groups, the rivalry over scarce urban regeneration funding, and poor local services, highlighted in Herman Ouseley's report on social fragmentation in Bradford.[11] It has also been deepened by the fear of difference and change, the hatred stimulated by racism, the growth in Islamophobia, and a general failure of political leadership. Asian community leaders are often out of touch with the younger generations. The White working class, part of Labour's heartlands, feel progressively detached from New Labour's modernizing project and, lacking progressive political leadership that would place local defensiveness in a broader context, are open to the seductions of racially activist minority parties such as the National Front and the British National Party.

Professor Ash Amin, summarizing extensive recent urban research, identifies two types of neighbourhood as typical of these degraded urban spaces:

The first are run down inner urban areas in which the conflict is between an old White working class lamenting the loss of a golden and ethnically homogenous past and non-White immigrants claiming a right of place, often against one another [. . .] The second type consists of 'White flight' suburbs and estates dominated by an aspirant working class or inward-looking middle class repelled by what it sees as the replacement of a homely White nation by another land of 'foreign' people and cultures. Here frightened families, White youths, and nationalist/Fascist activists disturbed by the fear (rarely the experience) of Asian and Black contamination terrorize a few immigrants and asylum seekers who happen to settle there.[12]

Both types of neighbourhood can be found in the new global/multicultural city. The former is the state of play in many so-called inner-city areas. The latter is more typical of the outer London suburbs such as Eltham into which Stephen Lawrence and his friend inadvisedly strayed looking for a bus home on the night when he was murdered by five white youths. In between, there are many mixed neighbourhoods up and down the country that seem relatively settled after years of patient negotiation, but which are nevertheless, in a subterranean and invisible way, 'riddled with prejudice and conflict between their varied ethnic groups' (Amin).

No longer 'the workshops of the world', English cities have become the service centres, the financial and speculative investment engines, and consumer retail hubs of the global economy. One after another, large cities—Leeds, Manchester, Bristol, Birmingham, Liverpool, and Newcastle as well, of course, as parts of London—have been revamped into transparent atrium-bedecked cosmopolises dominated by the corporate glass HQs of globally orientated enterprises. Surrounding the city bases of investment banking, entertainment, consumer retail, technology, and other corporate global giants are the sprawling satellites of outsourced service industries, both the 'producer services' (finance and investment, personnel, marketing, PR, advertising and media consultants, computer and design workshops) that provide the critical circuitry that knits the global economy together, and the consumer services that nourish the appropriate cultural tastes and lifestyles of its inhabitants.

The suited executives—those well-groomed, toned, and limousined corporate 'heroes' whose well-fleshed faces adorn the business pages of the quality newspapers and magazines—are either a new global entrepreneurial class or, alternatively, the remnants of an old stuffy one who have undergone a make-over. They are as at home in New York, Los Angeles, Hong Kong, Moscow, Kuala Lumpur, Tokyo, or Beijing as they are in Bishop's Avenue in London, in their country homes in Hampshire, or on their temporarily beached yachts at San Tropez. The gap between senior directors and CEOs has narrowed, since both have the same deep commitment to 'the business' and the 'bottom line', an overriding invest-ment in the nurturing of 'shareholder value', exorbitant six- or seven-figure salaries, reinforced by astronomical annual bonuses, generous share-option deals, private medical cover, and copper-bottomed retirement and pension schemes. Indi-vidually, their fortunes seem to rise and fall with surprising regularity, scandal and failure crowning meteoric rise as night follows day. But, as a class, they are installed as the permanent executive officers of the new global capitalism.

Many wealthier executives now live well outside the city or in its increasingly gated enclaves and pied-à-terres. They too are more cosmopolitan in orientation. They travel constantly for work and pleasure. They remain in touch, through the circuits of instant communication, with mobile transnational elites elsewhere as they glide in comfort and style across the globe. In contrast with their predecessors, they know much more about business and finance, marketing and PR, man-agement buy-outs, and branding than they know about pro-ducing, building, or making anything. They too are at home anywhere, and the more so since 'elsewhere' is increasingly like 'here', only more so. They are focused on profit mar-gins and share values, on restructuring core-businesses and absorbing other companies by merger and takeover. They are remorselessly attuned—and without a shadow of embarrass-ment—to salary settlements unrelated to any calculable per-formance achievements, guaranteeing the steady supply of staggering amounts of money for skiing holidays and private school fees. Their wives are fully occupied ferrying the younger children in 4-by-4s, people carriers, or SUVs (Sports Utility Vehicles) to select and selective private schools, those launch-pads to success. Fitzjohns Avenue in north-west London (or what the fancy estate agents call 'Hampstead borders'), where there must be twelve or fifteen private primary schools and nurseries within a half-mile stretch of traffic-crammed road, is notorious with taxi drivers. For the school run brings an army of jeeps, with their ranch-like bumpers, some parked in driveways, others perched on the bank-sides, others still blithely reversing into oncoming traffic.

In terms of lifestyle, this new global executive class increasingly blends into and makes common cause with the new rich—the self-made tycoons, the celebrities, and the new 'flashocracy'—for whom key sites in the city function as stage, playground, and photo-opportunity. They are 'flash, fast, fun, feckless, and fantastically frivolous', as the editor of *Tatler*, Geordie Greig—who should know—describes them (*The Observer*, 6 June 2004). Powered by a Veblenesque resurgence of conspicuous consumption, the nouveaux riches are also attached to global rather than national itineraries, agendas, and hot spots: film festivals, fashion house openings, award ceremonies, opening nights, race meets, and so on. Rapidly trading tweed for bling, they are experts in visualizing for the rest new forms of urban style and status: not 'status' as an alternative to 'class', as in the old Marx vs. Weber dialogue, but status as the cultural signifier of new riches, as the materialization of social success. They, too, are beginning to impose their tastes, ideas, and lifestyles on the global city.

The 'creatives' who service this corporate and celebrity world are very different in background and in attitudes to the older professional and managerial middle-classes. They are more individualistic, consumer-oriented, culturally savvy, lifestyle focused, entrepreneurial, and hedonistic. More often they are on fast-track mobility or aspirational escalators from lower in the social order. Here, rather than higher up the urban pecking order, the leading edge of the rising Asian and Afro-Caribbean new middle classes are beginning to carve out an elegant niche. The places they aspire to live in, the lifestyles they covet, and the kinds of leisure pursuits and entertainment they invest in are very different to older, more puritan tastes. Far from moving to the suburbs for a quiet life in respectable surroundings (later on in life they may, of course, buy a renovated barn or two in the country for weekends), they are the advance party of the new urban living—the agents of the 'gentrification' of older working-class residential areas and of industrial small-manufacturing dockland or storage areas of the city, whose abandoned warehouses, refashioned into loft-spaces and city-centre 'pads', they are rapidly colonizing. Good food, art galleries, smart cafés, and health-clubs are the necessary accompaniments to this lifestyle. These are the pioneers of an intense, designer-shaped, global consumerism, the avid readers of upmarket style magazines and celebrity supplements, and the cultural happy few exquisitely attuned to every minor shift or wobble in global postmodern taste and design.

At the other end of the scale are the poor areas that surround this vibrant 'global' centre. Some until very recently were 'the inner city'. But as city centres are increasingly trendified and colonized for urban nightlife and clubbing, their older inhabitants have increasingly been pushed to migrate towards the outer ring. In London, this means Harlesden, Cricklewood, Wembley, Southall, Tottenham, Haringey, and Tower Hamlets: *White Teeth* or *Brick Lane* territory. These are areas of mixed residency in which the new multiculturalism is being tested in a myriad everyday encounters. Here the better housing is highly sought after by professionals harried by ferociously rising house prices and land values. But these are typically areas of high and multiple disadvantage, with poor schools, forbidding estates, run-down or boarded-up high streets, high crime and drug rates, and drab terraces. They are often dilapidated, poorly serviced, and grim in terms of the conditions of life they offer. Increasingly, these are the colonized areas of immigrant settlement, whether by the first (Afro-Caribbean), second (Asian subcontinent: Indian, Pakistani, and Bangladeshi), third (West African, Turkish, and Greek Cypriot), fourth (North African: Somali, Sudanese, Moroccan, Algerian, etc.), fifth (Bosnian, Albanian, and Kosovan), sixth (Afghan, Iraqi, and Middle Eastern), or seventh (post-Soviet East European) migrant waves.

In these areas, white residents—who now feel threatened by change, abandoned by modernizing and multicultural political agendas, and neglected because they lack the entrepreneurial and 'creative' skills which the new service economy demands—meet the 'ethnic minority communities', whether in their young posse, trapped-and-deprived, veiled and turbaned or in their aspirational, socially and occupationally mobile manifestations. Corner grocery shops, greengrocers', market stalls, record shops, newsagents, minicab firms, small under-the-bridge mechanics and car-repair yards, cafés and fast-food late-night outlets are the small 'motors' of the local high-street economy of these city enclaves. The inner city, as the urbanists remind us, is a servicing-oriented economy too, a place of markets, exchange, the vigorous trading of goods and services, and the exploitation of niches—though at a much more depressed, small-scale, and marginal level than those described above.

Occasionally, there are small sweat-shops. These are patriarchal havens where migrant owners oversee a workforce composed largely of migrant female labour working at marginal rates of pay to produce designer 'versions', imitation branded goods, and fake fashion items for the street stalls. Family and female labour are the working backbone of these communities. Some (especially black women and educated second-generation Asians), by dint of enormous struggle and further education or training achieved at considerable personal and financial cost, manage to find a niche in the wider economy or are drawn into local government and the health and welfare services. If the men have steady work outside shop and home, it is often in transport. The more recent arrivals are overwhelmingly illegals: so-called economic migrants and asylum-seekers working at below minimum wages, washing up in cafés or on building sites, or brutally dragooned into the sex trade. Here, economic survival and family stability are tenuous, difficult accomplishments, and survival strategies, whether legal or illegal, are at a premium. 'Hustling', within or at the margins of the law, is the name of the game.

Some of these areas continue to function as 'transition zones' in which different groups interact and in which a sort of multicultural diversity is, here and there, beginning to appear on the ground. You see black and white groups at street corners, mixed-race couples in the local clubs and pubs, Asian shopkeepers and greengrocers who have become familiar local figures, the acceptance of a multi-ethnic, multicultural reality as the normal form of 'the local'. As the Parekh Report on *The Future of Multi-Ethnic Britain* observed:

Post-migration communities are distinct cultural formations but they are not cut off from the rest of British society [. . .] These communities are not and have never aspired to be separate enclaves. They are not permanently locked into unchanging traditions, but interact at every level with mainstream social life, constantly adapting and diversifying their inherited beliefs and values in the light of the migrant experience.[13]

Les Back has charted how, in some largely black areas of South London and elsewhere, a certain genuine cultural syncretism is emerging among young people in which music and urban street-style are critical zones of interchange, not only cementing a 'new ethnic' urban lifestyle among black and Asian youth, but drawing in a section of white 'wannabes'—Estuary/patois fluent, garage or drum-and-bass music aficionados.[14] In many ways, these longer-standing communities, which have negotiated a sort of truce with the dominant society that enables them to operate effectively while remaining in touch with community habits and values, are also part of an emerging transnational trend and belong to global urban formations. This is globalization from below. The syncretic forms of Black and Asian urban culture, especially, are integrated into informal and largely invisible city-to-city global cultural 'flows' in music, fashion, and street-style as well as drugs, from Kingston to Brixton and Harlesden to Queens and Brooklyn in New York to Manchester, to the Compton district in Los Angeles, to Atlanta, and on to the Berlin, Stockholm, and Warsaw club scenes.

However, other patterns exist and may be becoming stronger. Professor Amin is certainly right to warn that 'inter-ethnic understanding is not guaranteed by cultural hybridization'.[15] In some areas, the minority ethnic and 'host' communities live relatively separate lives, with everyday public exchanges conducted in a spirit of live and let live. In still other localities, not very far away from these, the local populations—young and old—have fallen apart into a silent but sullen separateness, a hostile and mutual defensiveness. Here, an embattled 'little

Englandism' has won vital sympathetic space within white urban working-class culture, and those perceived as outsiders on a number of criteria, of which skin colour is only one, really are at risk. This is especially true of recently arrived 'asylums'. Since the moral panic about the politicization of Islam, 9/11, and the 'war on terror', Islamophobia is everywhere close to the surface, and young Muslim men and women are particularly vulnerable.

It is clear that as we try, however roughly and impressionistically, to map the connections between the changing social and spatial configurations of the city and the new and emerging forces of globalization, a more complex picture of the 'global city' emerges. It is a city of more multiple and overlapping spaces, with complex patterns of interaction and the distribution of activities, resources, and attitudes. Diverse practices are to be found coexisting in the same urban spaces. However, divisions have also become more intense and entrenched. The reality is and for a long time has been that multiculturalism and racism proceed hand in hand. Indeed, in some ways these tendencies are becoming deeper, more entrenched, and wider in scope. But they do not mark the face of the city in such clear ways. The global city is more one of an intricate network of differences, any of which can at any time be activated as a potentially explosive line of division. In the global/ multicultural city, as Bridge and Watson argue, 'differences and identities are constituted in multiple and complex ways in multiple spaces of the city and shift and change, producing different city spaces and new boundaries and borders'.[16]

The history of post-war racism, as it relates to migration, has not been seriously studied. Popular and public attitudes in the early post-war years—migration in the shadow of decolonization and the 'end of empire'—were deeply implicated in the legacies of slavery, indenture, and colonization: they were still, broadly speaking, routed through the imperial connection. This involved the subordination of colonized economies to the advantage of the metropole—a fact visible in 'imperial' cities such as Bristol, Cardiff, and Liverpool—and was also reflected in the symbolic role the imperial idea played in the construction of British identity as a master and governing 'race'. This civilizational superiority became deeply woven into—and remains an active trace within—a post-imperial consciousness. It was very much to the fore in the early confrontations between native and migrant people. However, as the tides of migration broadened and settlement became more permanent and extensive, a profound shift occurred. To the degraded repertoires of race and colour were added other dimensions of racialized otherness more to do with cultural differences—historical, religious, linguistic, enshrined in custom, dress, familial practices and values, and so on—in the racialized system which came to be known as 'the new racism'. Since then, racialization of difference has increasingly drawn on these two repertoires, biogenetic and cultural.[17] Recently, migration flows into the UK, driven in connection with new developments in globalization, have broadened even further into multiple and diverse streams. Far from easing the associated tensions, a more complex overlapping system of civilizational differences has come into play alongside the older racialized repertoires, producing what Wieviorka and others call 'differential racism': a racism of racialized differences complexly articulated in relation to, but also between, different groups.

What promise, then, do these new urban patterns and formations hold out for a just and progressive resolution to the questions of social justice, equality, and diversity? The prospects are not optimistic. A kind of 'cosmopolitanism' does exist in the new elite spaces and formations of the global/multicultural city, because these spaces are now extensively connected with and orientated towards the wider world and its networks and agencies. However, this kind of cosmopolitan outlook has strict limits. Its principal effect is to reproduce within the city the divisions which globalization in its contemporary forms assumes in the wider world. Although the term 'globalization' has benefited greatly from its positive associations with an earlier version of 'internationalism', it has very little to do with distributing the wealth and resources of the planet to humanity in general in a more universal and egalitarian manner. Globalization is planetary in its scope, global in its operations. It creates and depends upon greater interdependence between different parts of the globe. But it and the elites it has created form a system rooted in power relations, driven by the imperatives and interests of the developed Western world, and grounded in the massive disparities of wealth and power between the world's rich and poor, the most critical dimension of which remains that between the West and its subalterns, and the Rest. Its principal effects are, largely, to exploit and reproduce these divisions and differences within the global city. Despite its implied promise of a better future for all, globalization is thus a highly contradictory system. For, as a sort of excess effect of the system or an unintended consequence, globalization 'from below' is also the site of a proliferation of differences which refuse to be corralled into a single unitary formation. This contradiction between the drive to political, economic, and cultural homogenization and the subaltern proliferation of difference across the globe is deeply unresolved by globalization in its contemporary form.

Of course, everybody is now being progressively drawn into the net of global investment, consumption, and technology. In this sense, a planetary cultural homogenization is making deep inroads. The new urban elites, and the parts of the city connected with them, have been pulled into its orbit. But resources, opportunities, and life-chances are not being levelled or equalized across the globe or within the city just because the system no longer has any real or effective 'outside'. The workers producing runner beans in East Africa for Western supermarkets are part and parcel of a global system of production, but that has no effect in equalizing their miserable rates of pay. The logging companies driving through the Amazonian forests may be dragging indigenous people into the web of globalization, but in the process they are also destroying the livelihoods and ecologies of those very people and laying waste to planetary resources.

For a time, at the other end of the scale, a sort of 'practical' multiculturalism seemed to offer a viable alternative. This was globalization from below—against the grain and logic of, and often in the very teeth of, globalization from above—though, as we have shown, still clearly articulated to its effects. Cosmopolitan in any simple sense it was not, for it was rooted in the significance and persistence of differences that refused to be homogenized into a planetary cultural consumerism, Western style. But it seemed for a time as if these were genuine differences which safeguarded the historical routes, memories, trajectories, and traditions that had sustained people and their ways of life through the terrible vicissitudes and dislocations of migration. These differences needed not to be subscribed to in a rigid, essentialist, doctrinal, or fundamentalist way and could, in the right circumstances, begin to be 'traded' and translated into broader, more inclusive patterns, as people with different histories who had come to the Western metropolis by different routes learned to live with and negotiate the terms on which they could occupy the same spaces as one another. The hope was that this might eventually give rise to forms of 'vernacular cosmopolitanism'.

However, the more globalization is harnessed to global systems of economic, military, and geopolitical power, the more it has become, in its dominant form, an integrated, expansionist, and missionary system. It obliges everyone to come into line with it and thus aims, by assimilation or forced conformity, to universalize itself; it makes its claims to universality come 'true' by ensuring that it is universal (or global) in its real operations and effects. Interventions in foreign places around the globe are no longer made just to safeguard Western interests but in the name of 'Western values', in President Bush's terms, and in order to bring 'freedom' to mankind and to liberate the world by making it 'just like us'.[18] In the UK in recent months, in the context of the 'war on terror', the adventure in Iraq, and rising new immigration numbers, multiculturalism, which for a time was official government doctrine, has been undermined and subverted as an ideal by spokespersons in and near to New Labour. It is being quietly buried. As the barriers to migration across Europe have become more entrenched, the pursuit of illegal immigrants more vigorous, and the policing of borders more systematic, so a widespread assimilationism not seen in the UK since the 1970s is rising to the surface and becoming de rigueur. Often it seems to proceed—paradoxically—under the cover of the call for social cohesion. Naturally, the enemies of this global universalism throughout the world have become more entrenched in their differences, and are now being represented as antithetical to 'modernity' (or

Western-dominated globalization), primordial, essentialist, untranslatable, and fundamentalist.

The global/multicultural city is being spatially and socially reconfigured by these processes and forces and, at the same time, becoming one of the critical sites where these contradictory tendencies, conflicts, and trajectories are being worked through. The city cannot resolve the wider contradictions of the globalization movement it reflects and embodies. But it will continue to be a sensitive recording template of the panoptic recomposition of power that is taking place as 'the global' continues to make its decisive mark.

2

Introduction to
Patricia J. Williams

Jane Shaw

The brilliance of Patricia Williams's work lies in her ability to use the personal to analyse the structures and institutions that affect our ways of living together. She has an unerring eye for the telling story which reveals to us our habits of being. As one of the foremost public intellectuals in the United States, she brings the qualities of a great and witty storyteller to her training as a lawyer, and tells us about ourselves.

In her books *The Alchemy of Race and Rights* (1991) and *The Rooster's Egg* (1995), she reveals the institutional racism that seeps through American society, corroding human rights on a day-to-day basis in ways both large and small. She shows how popular notions of racial difference are transmitted through American culture in myths about black single mothers and about America as a 'colour-blind' land of opportunity and hard work. She analyses the media's sensational reporting of African-Americans in positions of authority and of crimes involving black people. At the heart of such myths and media sensationalism, she argues, is a crippling fear of the other which divides societies against themselves, to everyone's loss and no one's gain.

It is this sense—that fear impedes and destroys civil rights and humiliates individuals on a daily basis—which drives the analysis she offers of American civil and urban society at this peculiar time of the 'war on terror' in her Oxford Amnesty Lecture. Beginning with the notion that America has a very particular notion of division within cities, one which is rooted in its own settler history where good and evil are seen to be battling for control, she then describes the present crisis as a structural problem masquerading as a personal one. Urban chaos is seen as 'the result [. . .] of personal choice to side with darkness'. Consequently, the threat of terrorism within America is viewed as one that is to be confronted by 'the project of rooting out the Evil-doers among us'. This is 'an enterprise in which the application of due process and sub-stantive justice is subordinated to a kind of secularized casting-out-of-demons from the Beloved Community'.

Williams reveals, in this way, the paradox of contemporary American society: human rights are asserted, declared the bedrock of democratic ideals, acclaimed as cherished in the daily rituals of life, and at the very same time endangered by panic and fear, such that 'the balance of freedom and security [will] tip too far toward the latter'. Williams's analysis of a string of recent cases in the USA, where people's rights (sim-ply to have access to a lawyer, for example) have been sus-pended, is devastating: the handling of these cases amounts to 'nothing less than the substitution of a presumption of guilt for the presumption of innocence'. She pinpoints the difficul-ties of finding a legal basis for this new, loose talk about terror-ism. The notion of a 'war on terror' makes war a broader concept than we have known before and allows its ways of being to creep into civil society and into the city. It also makes the boundaries between national and international more problematically porous. Williams's choice of exemplary story is, as always, witty and to the point, nowhere more so than in her reminder to us that, 'in its ongoing search for the leaders of the Ba'ath regime in Iraq, our [the US] Defense Department has issued a deck of bad-guy PLAYING cards, of all things'. She continues: 'if what US General Vincent Brooks said was literally true—that those pictured were to be "pursued, killed or captured"—then this "collectable" deck is little more than a gussied-up hit list'.

Williams reads this present situation through the lens of America's history of racialized struggle in which the temptation to 'string 'em-up' meant that 'police departments [. . .] looked the other way when the local bully boys decided that this or that black or Jewish or Catholic miscreant had looked the wrong way at a white woman or stolen a chicken or otherwise threatened the social order'. Then, she says, September 11 happened: 'suddenly the fear spread past Harlem, past South central, past the South Side. Round 'em up went global.' The danger, says Williams, is that in its hunger for catharsis after the trauma of 9/11, America may lose its sense of public accountability and thus the very freedoms and rights it cherishes.

What is to be done? In her Reith Lectures, delivered in Britain in 1997, and published as *Seeing a Colour-Blind Future: The Paradox of Race* (1997), Williams not only analysed American society but also turned the spotlight on us, that is, British (primarily white) society. The media reaction was predictably hysterical, whether on Radio 4's *Start the Week* programme or in the *Daily Mail*. What she is trying to tell us as a society, if we would but listen, is that we cannot have the colour-blind society we liberals so desperately wish we had until we face up to our own racism. We have to account for who we are and what we do. The personal is related to the structural. Colour-blindness is a legitimate hope for the future, but first we require accountability—and this is what she calls for here in the 'war on terror' as it is being fought in America's divided cities. Williams does not leave us without hope. Her analysis may be biting, but at the heart of her work there is always a vision of what *could* be, starting with the rightful application of human rights, as enshrined in the American constitution, to all people. For this bright new future of justice and peace, we require not only the putting aside of fear, not only public and private accountability, but also imagination and creativity, the possibility of jumping over the breach into a new world. This is how she put it in the first of her Reith Lectures:

And what a *good* thing it is, is it not, to try to imagine how much better we could be . . .

'I had a dream' said my son the other morning. Then he paused. 'No' he said, 'it was more of a miracle. Do you know what a miracle is?'

'Tell me,' I said, thunderstruck, and breathless with maternal awe.

'A miracle is when you have a dream and you open your eyes in it. It's when you wake up and your dream is all around you.'

It was a pretty good definition, I thought. And even though my son's little miracle had something to do with pirates meeting dinosaurs, I do think that to a very great extent we dream our worlds into being. For better or worse, our customs and laws, our culture and society are sustained by the myths we embrace, the stories we recirculate to explain what we behold. I believe that racism's hardy persistence and immense adaptability are sustained by a habit of human imagination, deflective rhetoric, and hidden licence. I believe no less that an optimistic course might be charted, if only we could imagine it.

Theatres of War

Patricia J. Williams

The theme of these Lectures immediately called to mind *A Tale of Two Cities*, with its tension between hysteria and reason; then I thought about *The Merchant of Venice*'s dual systems of justice, in which bargains were sealed either by a pound of flesh or by the exchange of wedding vows. Then I heard our Secretary of Defense, Donald Rumsfeld, dismissing complaints about the disorder in Iraq by observing that the death rate in the city of embattled Baghdad was actually less than that in purportedly peaceful Washington DC: 'If Washington DC were the size of Baghdad, we would be having something like 215 murders a month,' he said, as though to soothe.[1] I don't know why he supposed this might make anyone feel better about anything, but it did provide great grist for the purposes of this lecture.

Let me start by discussing what I think is at the symbolic root of a peculiarly American conception of division within cities, as well as between inner cities and their outer suburbs. From the time of the first Puritan settlers, the battle between chaos and form, dark and light, good and evil, was at the centre of all discourse. Historian Sacvan Bercovitch has written extensively about how that Puritan 'errand into the wilderness' has shaped much of the political rhetoric of the United States since.[2] The theme of divided cities was embedded in those early sermons in an almost physical sense. To those settlers, there was not just a conceptual distinction between right and wrong, but a literal, even geographic one. Those stern and rugged founding fathers envisioned establishing a shining city on a hill; the New World was figured as their New Jerusalem.

John Bunyan's seventeenth-century epic *The Pilgrim's Progress* is perhaps better known to a British audience for the kinds of images that framed that Puritan world: in particular, the notion of a chaotic, lawless City of Destruction as one option on life's road, the gleaming promise of a hard-won Celestial City as the alternative. One can sense the power of this vision made literal in the expressions of a range of present-day American political leaders: that each of us bears a terrible burden of sin we must counterbalance by doing good work. That there are Evil Powers in the world, often disguising themselves as allies. That urban chaos, whether in Washington DC or Baghdad, Iraq, is the result of personal freedom, in other words, of individual choice to side with darkness, rather than a sign of structural deficit. That the straight and narrow path toward the Celestial City is to be pursued with missionary zeal, despite seemingly insurmountable obstacles, and despite what everyone else on earth might say.

Admirable as such resolve might be as an abstract matter, I worry that such a world-view allows one to neglect the cost of real structural or institutional problems, as well as downplay the advice of any voice other than that of one's personal convictions. The project of routing out 'the Evildoers' among us, moreover, risks becoming an enterprise in which the application of due process and substantive justice is subordinated to a kind of secularized casting-out-of-demons from the Beloved Community. It is by something like this logic that the complicated phenomenon of Camp X-Ray at Guantanamo Bay has come into existence, as well as a whole series of so-called 'end-runs' around the American court system.

Like many Americans, like many American lawyers in particular, I am deeply troubled by this trend. I worry it can lead only to greater divisions among ourselves, within our communities, and in the world beyond.

There was a joke circulating on the internet not long ago. A grandmother overhears her 5-year-old granddaughter play-acting a wedding. The wedding vows go like this: 'You have the right to remain silent. Anything you say may be held against you. You have the right to have an attorney present. You may kiss the bride.'

I love this joke because it so brilliantly expresses the degree to which assertion of rights is a paramount ritual of American life. Yes, it is a parody of the supposed litigiousness of American society, a tweak at the litany every schoolchild learns not in school but from television police dramas. But it does capture the symbolic centrality of the freedoms and protections guaranteed by the United States Constitution, that structure so specifically designed to protect us from excessive power and arbitrary witch-hunts.

We Americans have all grown up knowing the catechism. 'Ask for a lawyer immediately upon your arrest.' The informational card the American Civil Liberties Union hands out to citizens is entitled 'What To Do If You're Stopped By The Police'. It is a list of rights we have long taken for granted, with advice about how to behave in a manner consistent with expectations of minimal due process. 'Try to find witnesses,' it continues. 'Ask if you are under arrest. If you are, you have a right to know why.'

Unfortunately, that little litany has been facing serious ridicule in some quarters of late, scoffed at as antiquated in comparison to shiny new notions that promise fast-track delivery of expedited justice. And so the assumption of innocence until proved guilty is under attack as inefficient in an era of terrorism. The right to a lawyer, so essential in holding the state to its burden of proof, is under attack as an indulgent frill subsidized by the terminally naive. Even the very option of a trial is being questioned as many Americans have begun to reconfigure all criminality as a species of active warfare. The Justice Department's own inspector general published a scathing critique of the 'unstated policy' that has allowed the FBI to detain illegal immigrants indefinitely until 'it was established that they were not tied to terrorism'.[3]

To a large extent this new cynicism is driven by deep fear. It is understandable given our newly heightened sense of an embattled world. But that is what our Constitution has always been there for: to act as a buffer in times when we are driven by fear, too tempted by the easy promise of rough-'n-ready justice. Moreover, those Constitutional safeguards embody the best traditions of Anglo-American jurisprudence. *Habeus corpus*, due process, the body of civil rights, and by extension, human rights: these represent the very core of our shared values, the bedrock of our democratic ideals.

The fear that I wish to articulate here is that some part of that shared tradition is endangered as never before by the panic of these times. I am aware that this is a wild and dangerous world. But I am also afraid that we will lose what is most precious in our democracy if we allow the balance between freedom and security to tip too far toward the latter.

I trust it will not be entirely uninteresting if I write mostly about American policies, cases, and actions; that is what I know. But I offer my thoughts assuming that, perhaps increasingly, trends in America parallel what goes on in Britain. I offer these thoughts because I am alarmed by some of the overly-broad provisions of new anti-terrorism laws that have been enacted in both our nations. I offer these few words in the hope that they will be of some use in our shared debate about the nature of any emergency we face, and about the range of legitimate measures to be pursued by our besieged leaders.

Let me start with a recent court case. On 8 January 2003, an American judge, sitting in our Fourth Circuit Court of Appeals, ruled that Yassir Hamdi, an American citizen captured in Afghanistan, could be held indefinitely, without charge and without access to a lawyer. The judge in the case ruled that the 'the courts are ill-positioned to police the military's distinction between those in the arena of combat who should be detained and those who should not'.

While the court's ruling explicitly applies to 'enemy combatants' captured in the 'theatre of war', it also limits the scope of judicial inquiry as to precisely what those terms might mean. In other words, not only can Hamdi have no lawyer, he cannot challenge his designation as enemy soldier, nor even whether the war was or is still going on. Such determinations, said the court, are solely within the discretion of the President and his military advisers. The Fourth Circuit's decision came on the heels of a case brought by Jose Padilla, another American citizen, captured not on the battlefield but in O'Hare airport in Chicago, Illinois.

Padilla has been in a military brig for nine months at the time of writing without any formal charge (although John Ashcroft's Justice Department has publicized its conviction that he was planning to detonate a so-called dirty bomb). Padilla also challenged his designation as an enemy combatant; and, early last December, a federal District Court judge held that 'Padilla's need to consult a lawyer is obvious'. That ruling, however, which was widely interpreted as one protecting a modicum of Padilla's due process, still leaves him without the right to a lawyer present during interrogation. And it is during interrogation, according to very disquieting reports in newspapers on both sides of the Atlantic, that so-called 'low-level' forms of torture are sometimes being employed, such as sleep deprivation, 'mild' roughing up, then deportation to countries such as Egypt and Morocco where 'real' torture is used.

Ultimately, the courts will have to chart some more consistent course in the cases now cropping up since September 11. After all, a third man, John Walker Lindh, was also an American citizen captured on a battlefield in Afghanistan, but he was tried in US courts. His case was attended by a near-universal public sense that, for purposes of his situation, the war had ended when Hamid Karzai took power.

What is at least as worrisome as the inconsistency is that the Bush administration has repeatedly defended its power to detain enemy combatants not simply in the war against Al Qa'eda or Afghanistan or Iraq or North Korea but 'in this war on terror'. This phrasing means that war is suddenly a much broader concept than we have known before. For example, you may have heard about the sniper shootings that paralysed Washington, Maryland, and Virginia in the autumn of 2002. Two citizens were captured, a juvenile and his abusive, reclusive stepfather. There seems to be no question that they acted alone and for deeply idiosyncratic, dare I say crazy reasons, rather than for any political end (although much has been made of the stepfather's mental problems, apparently a result of stress suffered during his military service in the 1992 Iraq war). Yet prosecutors sparked heated controversy when they proposed charging the juvenile, John Lee Malvo, under an anti-terrorism statute. Does this mean that Malvo's quite terrifying but wholly domestic crimes have the potential to turn suburban Washington DC into a theatre of war?

While I'm not at all sure that Malvo's alleged crimes fall into the category of what we mean by political terrorism, they did, without doubt, inspire mass fear. But consider the recent case of a 17-year-old boy travelling with his parents and sister, on their way to a Hawaiian vacation. He was arrested at Boston's Logan airport and charged in federal court with making a bomb threat. The teenager, evidently annoyed at the system of 'randomly' searching checked bags, had left a note in his suitcase that read: '**** you. Stay the **** out of my bag, you ****ing sucker. Have you found a ****ing bomb yet? No, just clothes. Am I right? Yea, so **** you.'[4] This case worries me. While the young man was certainly foul-mouthed and furiously intemperate, it is, by the same token, rather typical adolescent hot-headedness. The note conveyed great anger at the invasion of privacy, but suggested no actual harm, made no actual threat. I am worried that, whether or not the case actually makes it all the way to trial, the very charge and its attendant publicity sets a new low threshold for felony charges in the war against terror.

The fact is the United States hasn't officially declared 'war' against anyone. The Bush administration's commitment to end terror is a good thing, but terror is neither a three-dimensional enemy nor a clearly defined legal concept. It is more like a poison leaching from a deep well. The clean-up could take decades. Identifying the source and composition is likely to be a nightmare that may never be satisfactorily or completely resolved. 'Terror' defies scientific description. Surely we ought to have some more refined legal reference point than that.

In Padilla's case, moreover, we are dealing with someone who was planning to act, but who had not yet acted. Without evidence sufficient to file charges—if there is such, no one has yet produced it—the government has moved well into the area of prior restraint. This policy of detention based on John Ashcroft's or Donald Rumsfeld's secret 'convictions' about guilt rather than conviction by some accountable procedure like a trial—even if not entirely public—is a dangerous course.

This strategy is the logical if monstrous offspring of suspect profiling, which, when unsustained by evidence, is nothing less than the substitution of a presumption of guilt for the presumption of innocence. Without the legal counsel historically guaranteed, yes, even in military tribunals, we as citizens are licensing a shadow intelligence force that can hold people until they literally rot in jail, or can somehow prove themselves innocent without what is too often disparaged as the 'coaching' of lawyers. In President Bush's State of the Union speech of 28 January 2003, he directly addressed this newly expedited status of the presumptively guilty suspect: 'All told, more than three thousand suspected terrorists have been arrested in many countries. Many others have met a different fate. Let's just put it this way, they are no longer a problem to the United States and our friends and allies.' It is allusive, that reference to 'a different fate', the past tense of 'no longer a problem'.

Perhaps the President forgot that he was talking about suspected terrorists and not convicted war criminals. Maybe he meant not suspects but actual soldiers killed in combat or caught in the crossfire. Maybe that's what he meant: that they were active soldiers who met the sort of fate that is meted out on battlefields. But his allusiveness certainly suggests a bit more—the logic of guerrilla warfare applied to suspected enemies: 'eliminate the enemy, and don't let even the associates or families escape, because you can't trust ANYONE'. It is immensely careless in its sweep, too terribly capacious in its indictments.

By the same token, it chills me that, in its search for the leaders of the Ba'ath regime in Iraq, our Defense department issued a deck of bad-guy PLAYING cards, of all things. If what US General Vincent Brooks said was literally true—that those pictured were to be 'pursued, killed or captured'—then this 'collectable' deck is little more than a gussied-up hit list. As such, the poker-styled playfulness trivializes what those with no sense of humour might carelessly interpret as our own home-grown fatwa. It was chilling to hear commentators speak, not of Saddam Hussein's death, but of 'taking out the ace of spades'. The taking of any life, even those of sworn enemies, demands solemnity and careful account. We must add to the list of mounting concerns the continuing failure of both the British and American governments to account for Iraqi casualties. If we speak of 'acceptably low' casualties for our side, must we not think about what would be an 'unacceptably high' toll on the other? A hundred, a hundred thousand, a million? We wanted to prevent the proliferation of weapons of mass destruction. Given the extraordinary superiority of our military force, does not morality demand that we ourselves not wreak massive destruction, massive injury, massive loss of life? We must know these things.

The unexplained dispatch of those deemed 'a problem' is perhaps a simple matter of diction, reflective of a kind of *Terminator*-style Hollywood glibness to which our present leaders seem attracted. But it is alarmingly similar to the kind of deadly code by which too many human rights crises in recent history have been winked away. In *Prisoner Without a Name, Cell Without a Number*, Jacobo Timerman describes how middle-class Argentinians and the intelligentsia indulged in both complacency and denial despite evidence of mounting numbers of the 'disappeared' during the junta in that country. They too were assured by representations that there was 'no problem'. Similarly, Vidal-Naquet's book *La Torture dans la République* documents the covert killings of Algerian revolutionaries carried out by the Parisian police.[5]

Such dispatch of persons deemed suspicious is officially premised on a cost–benefit analysis that rationalizes the sacrifice of a few to save the many. But this logic, when practised outside situations of extreme or battlefield emergency, licenses behaviour that squanders the good will of whole populations. There is no shortcut to justice. This logic explains why African-Americans who would love good policing in their neighbourhoods frequently end up as frightened of the police as of the neighbourhood thugs. I think it also explains why polls in South Korea suddenly indicate more fear of the United States than of North Korea.

Indeed, a recent human rights report says that the global campaign against terrorism is weakening because of the Bush administration's own human rights excesses as well as its willingness selectively to overlook the abuses of its allies. The message that 'human rights are dispensable in the name of fighting terrorism' is, according to some analysts, actually fuelling anti-American sentiment. I am so worried that this foolish path will cost us more than it gains; it can lead to nothing but yet more sadness, yet more paradox.

Let me return to the complications raised by President Bush's expedited fate for suspected terrorists. A recent letter to the editor of the *New York Times* focused on Bush's seeming 'implication that the murder of suspects in such circumstances is not only allowable but a thing to be proud of. What would happen,' asked the letter writer, 'to the police chief of a large city if he declared that "suspected terrorists" were being dispatched in such a manner?'

It's a good question, really. What indeed would happen if the police disposed of suspected criminals with a cryptic 'Let's just say they're no longer a problem . . .'? But the practices of overzealous policing and quickie backroom punishment meted out by police and police alone were, in a way, all part of what was at stake in the civil rights movement in the United States. There was a long history in the segregated south of police departments that looked the other way when the local bully boys decided that this or that black or Jewish or Catholic miscreant had looked the wrong way at a white woman or stolen a chicken or otherwise threatened the social order.

Overzealous policing and the careless employ of lethal force are pivotal elements in understanding why we had so many urban riots at a certain point in our history, and why we continue to struggle with a range of very troubling scandals today. This temptation to 'string-'em-up' bedevils law enforcement in any culture or context. In the United States it has been an unfortunately racialized struggle given the sad history of segregation. (Segregation itself of course is yet another grand idea purporting to preserve the social order.) So we've had hearing after hearing in city after city. The funny thing is that we do know how to fix the problem if only we have the will. With greater accountability, better training, more respect and, most of all, the appropriate administration of due process, have come greater peace, better relations, more trust.

'Efficiency' without careful investigation and balancing of

evidence is inherently prone to mistake and to bias, inherently short-sighted and corrupting. Yet, while knowing all this, we seem intent on tightening the overlap between the tactics of outright war and the practices of urban policing. During the search for the Washington DC area sniper, the FBI called in Army reconnaissance planes to try to find him. This was touted as a fair response under the circumstances, but in the process we Americans quietly witnessed the ultimate conflation of army and police.

Given the reorganization of police power since 9/11, it seems almost anti-climactic, reasonable, desirable; given the urgency of current events, we seem to have abandoned all thought of other, less constraining alternatives. Who needs gun control, goes the popular logic, when we can have the gloriously panoptic control of the military maintaining aerial surveillance of suburban shopping malls? And, people ask, is it really so different from those surveillance cameras that former New York City Mayor Rudolf Giuliani's administration installed all over Manhattan?

As an aside, it must be noted that Mayor Giuliani himself has been travelling around the world coaching urban police departments in ways to reduce crime. Recently he was hired by Mexico City, where he plans to follow the same formula he used in New York: targeting certain neighbourhoods and arresting every violator, no matter how minor, on the supposition that petty criminals are predisposed to larger crimes. It will be interesting to see how this works in Mexico City, so much of whose population is desperately poor, and so many of whom beg illegally. It will be interesting to see how much of the population ends up behind bars before some kind of crisis erupts. But let me not be a naysayer: Mexico City's leaders are so filled with bright hope about the possibility for turnaround that they have recently decided to outfit their street cops like cowboys, complete with large sombreros.

The image of police as global urban cowboys is no laughing matter. It was a self-described team of police 'cowboys' who shot Amadou Diallo, after all. Diallo was an unarmed African immigrant living in the Bronx; he had just emerged from the front door of his house and was standing on his top step when he was felled in a rain of forty-one bullets. The police were scared, it was later said. He moved the wrong way, perhaps reaching to get his wallet. They really didn't mean it.

It was the teach-'em-a-lesson justice of the Wild West, too, that motivated officers to assault Abner Louima, a Haitian immigrant, living in Brooklyn, who was mistaken for someone who had instigated a bar-room brawl. Louima was taken to the police precinct house and brutally assaulted by officers who rammed a broom handle up his rectum. In the light of great publicity, the officers were charged and convicted in that case. That is as it should be. But I worry: I cannot say with certainty that we would ever have known about Louima, particularly given his status as a non-citizen, if it had happened today. With broad new discretionary powers of all branches of law enforcement to arrest and detain suspects secretly and indefinitely, there might never have been a public outcry, we might never have known of that secret sadism committed in our names.

The need for openness, however messy, is not limited to the extremes of misbehaviour. Informed public accountability (as opposed to ill-informed media entertainment) keeps us informed of our fallibilities and cautious and humble in the endeavour of presuming to know all. It was a street crimes unit under intense, at times hysterical, public pressure to make New York safe for tourism that led to the arrest and conviction of five young men in the so-called 'Central Park Jogger' case. In 1991, a young stockbroker was jogging in Central Park at about 9 o'clock at night. She was brutally beaten and raped and very nearly died. The jogger remembered nothing. The police arrested five African-American teenagers, some as young as 14, who had been in the park at some point within twelve hours of the assault. Police obtained confessions from four out of the five although there was no other evidence to place them at what was an extremely bloody and muddy crime scene. All the young men were convicted. Their obligingly sullen faces were melded with the newly coined notion of 'wilding', that is, of rampaging 'young black males' who were taking over the city. That notion in turn justified a degree of racial 'profiling' on an unprecedented and now national scale. Only within the last few months has it come to public light that DNA evidence implicates a serial rapist who has confessed to committing the crime alone. The police department has hastily countered with a report insisting that the original jogger defendants must have been involved in something. But the police department's belief, however sincere, is no substitute for hard evidence. Their belief, however sincere, is why we keep things public, and put things to the test in a court of law, however imperfect.

Perhaps this is not an apt analogy for what is going on at the global level, but I am nagged by the question as posed in the letter section in the *New York Times*, of what happens if the police act as though they're at war, or when the executive branch of the most powerful nation on earth begins to employ the tactics of what we had, until very recently, agreed were corrupt backroom tactics of overly stressed urban policing. Perhaps it is not an apt analogy—I am not an expert in international affairs—but let me offer it anyway. We seem to be on the verge of what I fear will be a terribly vengeful era. And this is all I have to offer as a cautionary tale.

So allow me to spend just a moment more speaking about why I think the Central Park Jogger case is an instructive object lesson. First, the defendants did not have adequate representation. The defence attorneys were as incompetent as any I have ever seen, almost comically so. Their competence was challenged far too late, in a hearing on appeal.

Second, the defendants never should have been tried together. They were too easily depicted as a clotted unit, 'the' wilders, a singular pack, five individuals melded into one hyper-horrific presumptively suspect profile. If we think such imagery is not a factor in military tribunals, where access to counsel of one's choice is not provided, we are naive indeed.

Third, the confessions were questionable, and no one seemed to care. The confessions were preceded by 18 to 30 hours of non-stop questioning, sometimes under quite unorthodox circumstances. For example, one 14-year-old was put in the back of a police car and driven around the park in the middle of the night. Police didn't feel it necessary to translate every question into Spanish for the family of another for fear that it was 'going to take us all day'. The confessions themselves were filled with inconsistencies and obvious factual errors that no one has taken seriously until now. Most troubling, the first handwritten draft of the confessions was in police-speak. It seems that one detective wrote down three of the four incriminating confessions before they were videotaped. My notes of that detective's testimony reveal that he didn't 'know if I substituted Ramon's words for my own, but I wrote down what I recall'. The 'male black'? 'Probably my words.' 'Female white'? 'He probably said white female. Or white girl.' 'Had sex'? 'I don't recall if those were his words or mine.' Nor was the statement 'in exactly the same order that he told me'. If we think such practices will not be a far greater problem in interrogations of enemy combatants with no review at all, we are doubly naive.

Fourth, there was no physical evidence. Indeed, aside from the confessions, there was no evidence of any sort. This was an extraordinarily bloody crime—the jogger lost about three-quarters of the blood in her body—and the scene was a particularly muddy one. But there was no blood on any of the accused, nor were any of their footprints found at the scene.

Soil traces in their sneakers had a mineral content consistent with the ground in the entire upper half of Manhattan, but which the prosecution maintained 'proved' that they were in the park that night. While the district attorney, in her final argument, maintained that hairs from the jogger were found on two of the defendants, the actual testimony of the forensic analyst was never so conclusive. Rather, he said the hairs were more consistent with Caucasian hair than African-American. But this point sailed over the heads of many in the courtroom.

When I hear that many New Yorkers are still maintaining that these five young men were somehow involved in some criminal activity somewhere in the park that night, I hear the same sort of rationalizing that has fed such apathy to the more thoughtless of our anti-terrorism policies. In this as in all cases, if there is evidence of criminality, we should prosecute. But if there is no evidence, our suspicions, fears, and insinuations are no substitute. I appreciate the need to balance security against freedom, but in such cases, I worry that unlimited, secret, and unreviewed detentions are extremely short-sighted, self-serving, and in the long term as dangerous to democracy as terrorism itself. And I do not say that lightly.

In the Central Park Jogger case, the prosecutors were scared. The police were scared. The public felt 'terrorized' by crime in New York City. But in addressing it, something awful happened. Police started picking up anyone who frightened them. A majority of the public called for tough laws with fewer protections for defendants. Racial profiling told us who to be afraid of before they did anything. There was a vast public acceptance of bad police practices rendered by stressed, frightened, badly trained officers; and that is before we get to the rogue, bad-apple, openly corrupt policemen who have been the subject of scandals in New York, Los Angeles, Philadelphia, and Chicago. The result is a deep racial, cultural, and class divide, particularly between black and white. Both sides wanting protection; only one getting it.

Then September 11 happened. Suddenly the fear spread past Harlem, past South Central, past the South Side. Round 'em up went global.

It's a scary little world right now. Such wars of careless words. Such panic on every breeze. If Eskimos have a hundred words for snow, we have let bloom a thousand words for fear. What bitter tests between power and the ideal, what varied options for doom. Loss of freedom versus loss of security. Osama Bin Laden versus the CIA. Global warming versus economic collapse. Smallpox versus man-made strains of polio, mad cow versus West Nile virus. With such endless possibilities, we fear everything that moves.

Lots of people are thinking like this, we're told, in the inevitable trail of paranoia that fills the wake of great disaster. *New York Times* columnist Clyde Haberman recently wrote about a couple who took a dinner cruise around Manhattan. They became unnerved by a woman seated at the next table because she was by herself and 'extremely overdressed', 'seemed to be a foreigner', kept checking her watch, and carried a black canvas bag. The couple called the boat's manager to report her as 'suspicious' and to have that bag investigated. Nothing was out of order and the couple's concerns were dismissed as overwrought, but Haberman ended his column with all the dark drama of a mystery novel: 'This time it was a collection of random facts that add up to nothing. Still . . .'

It is the ominous 'Still . . .' that hangs over us all like a sickness.

Haberman's case, at least, did not end like the debacle in Florida where a Shoney's waitress overheard three 'Muslim-looking' men discussing their plans to 'bring down' something. She assumed they meant civilization or at least a few buildings. The police closed off a major highway for seventeen hours and blew up their knapsacks before it was learned that the men were only talking about bringing their car down to Florida.

Such great edginess eats away at our capacity to reason. A friend who is a teacher says that one of the questions they ask children on IQ tests is what they would do with a wallet if they found it on the street. The high-scoring answer is that you would find a police officer and hand it over. But black children, especially boys, almost never say that. They'd take it to their mothers or another female relative to have them turn it over. They tend to avoid police officers, and try not to have their names or that of any man they know in any public agency's files, especially those of the police. But taking the wallet to your mother in the race-blind context of standardized tests is a sign of immaturity. Little boys run to their mothers. Big, smart, fearless boys take things directly to the men in charge. Thus 'common' sense exists in complicated relation to value systems of coded fear and encrypted credibility.

As the fear that has gripped our nation metastasizes beyond the profiling that has so constrained ghetto life and spreads to women who eat alone in public places while checking their watches, I worry that we are all at risk of becoming more childlike, more intimidated, less able to deal straightforwardly with the big men in charge.

I feel this new tentativeness every time I fly. I flew to Philadelphia recently, and went through all the abasements of airport security, a ritual cleansing of the sort that until recently was practised only at the gates of maximum security prisons. I removed my shoes. 'Take off your coat,' they instructed. I held out my arms. We know there is good reason for it. We are polite. A guard in a rakish blue beret bestowed apologies like a rain of blessings as she wanded my armpits. 'Do you have an underwire in your bra?' she asked. 'You mind if I feel?' It is hard to be responsive to such a prayer with any degree of grace. It is ceremonial, I know. But I *do* mind. Yet I know I'll end up in strip-search hell if I go down that route. I was polite. I obeyed. 'Not at all,' I intoned, as though singing in Latin.

Over at another table, another agent was going through my bags. He removed my nail clippers from the intimacy of my make-up pouch and discarded them in a large vat filled with what seemed to be hundreds of small nail clippers. A proper sacrifice, I thought: I imagine they will distribute them to the poor. The agent put on rubber gloves and opened my stainless steel thermos and swirled the coffee around, peering into it with narrowed eyes. He removed the contents of my purse, spread it out, and asked me to turn on my Palm Pilot. When he picked up my leather-bound diary and flipped slowly through the pages, a balloon of irreligiosity exploded at the back of my head, and I could feel my hair rise up, as it does sometimes, getting militant despite my best prostrations of mousse. 'My diary?' I said as evenly as I could. 'This is getting to be like the old Soviet Union.' 'So, you visited the Soviet Union?' he asked, a glinty new interest hardening his prior languor.

Anyway, I finally got to where I was going. And on my way back from Philadelphia, I wasn't searched at all. They stopped the woman just in front of me, though, and there she stood, shoeless and coatless, with the tampons from her purse emptied upon the altar of a plastic tray. Once on the plane, she and I commiserated, and then the oddest thing happened. Others around us joined in about how invaded and humiliated they felt. The conversation spread across the aisle, then to the seat in front, the row in back. It grew to about five rows of people, all angry at the overseers, all suspicious, disgruntled, and afraid. I was, I admit, strangely relieved to see that we were not all black or brown; we were men and women, white and Asian, young kids, old designer suits. There was a weird, sad kind of unity in our vulnerability, in this helplessness of ours. But there was a scary emotional edge to the complaining, a kind of heresy that flickered through it too. What a baffled little coterie we were.

I worry about what goes into my trash bins. I reviewed my notes for my Oxford Amnesty Lecture before leaving the US. I combed through my words about how much I wish we could avoid war with Iraq to make sure that they could not be interpreted as an attempt unduly to influence US foreign policy sufficient to get me surveilled under Section 802 of the USA Patriot Act, which includes, in its definition of domestic terrorism, activities that 'appear to be intended to influence the policy of government by intimidation or coercion . . .' You have to be careful: just about everyone's feeling intimidated by something these days.

A friend of mine is a social worker who works with battered women. She observes that there is a syndrome among some of them in which they actually provoke their abusers into hitting them. Legally, of course, it doesn't make them less victims, nor the abusers less at fault. But as a psychological matter, it's interesting. However patently self-destructive it may be, instigating a fight is an attempt to control the terms of abuse. People who have been consistently battered suffer not only the injury of the actual beating, but extreme stress from not knowing when the next blow will fall. As irrational as it may seem from the outside, such provocation relieves that stress.

My friend the social worker said that she herself was feeling something like that urge in the weeks following the first anniversary of the September 11 attacks. Indeed, she attributed much of the American public's enthusiasm for war to this traumatized emotionalism, this hunger for catharsis. She acknowledged feeling much the same herself—this intolerable sense that the other shoe is just about to drop. 'I just want it to be OVER with!' she exclaimed in frustration, and loudly enough for a few heads to turn in the restaurant where we were having lunch. 'Shut up, or they'll pre-emptively blow up that Prada bag of yours,' I said, alarmed if overwrought.

Nothing happened. Everyone went on eating, perhaps recognizing that this was just a momentary lapse from civil society, the sort of thing that is bound to happen when we suffer our lives to be underwritten by the imagined worst or the worst imaginable. Still . . .

Sometimes things get so crazy that people simply cannot hear through the mass-driven fear of the moment. As we ride out the heightened troubles of these times, as our domestic fears become conflated with international terror, let us try hard not to fall back on the models that have betrayed us so often, those of cowboys, careless verbiage, and blind faith in the culture of guns.

If I'm right that we're in for a long stretch of backlash and retrenchment, what will matter most is the ability to endure the long-term powerlessness. What will matter now is how to be resilient, persistent, even when reform is not likely to come about for decades. Now is certainly a moment to build broader and more complex coalitions than we have seen in recent years, for the political forces with which we must grapple are broader and more complex. The technology of population control alone ensures that this will be so.

For example, the heretofore unknown Defense Advanced Research Projects Agency has generated considerable controversy with its plans to launch a computer system called Total Information Awareness that would profile a lot more Americans than just young black men. The system would have the capacity to scan, without search warrant, our emails, credit card, and banking statements, medical records, and travel records. It has been said they'll be searching for 'patterns' that suggest terrorist activity, a description that does not adequately convey the fear we ought to feel now that citizens are about to be surveilled not for law enforcement purposes but for military ends. Bear in mind that those computerized search engines are very much like spellcheckers in their search for 'pattern'. This morning I happened to type the name 'Amanda' in an email I was sending. The spellchecker wanted to know if I didn't mean 'armadillo'. I worry that the military's spellchecker will want to know if I didn't really mean 'armada'. Even without such a programme, the magazine *Business Week* reports that 'since September 11, various federal agencies, including the State Department, Customs Service, and FBI, have created lists of suspicious travellers, Americans and foreigners. All told, some 13 million people (equivalent to 4.5 per cent of the US population) are on the terror watch list. Security experts and common sense say 99 per cent of those pinpointed aren't terrorists.' One wonders what criteria they're using.

But we must not make the mistake of spending more time watching our words than those of our elected representatives, our leaders, our guardians. I am not so cynical as to doubt that our leaders are doing what they can in the midst of this ungodly global mess. Nor, on the other hand, am I so naive as to assume my few words are much more than a vain murmur in the face of events so overwhelming. But again, I speak not in vanity, but because I feel I must, as a deep believer in the obligations of citizenship, and as one who is committed to the fundamental values of democracy.

Let me end with playwright Arthur Miller's warning to us not to turn our civic engagement into a crucible where political opposition 'is given an inhumane overlay which then justifies the abrogation of all normally applied customs of civilized intercourse. A political policy is equated with moral right, and opposition to it with diabolical malevolence. Once such an equation is effectively made, society becomes a congeries of plots and counterplots, and the main role of government changes from that of the arbiter to that of the scourge of God.'[6]

3

Introduction to David Harvey

Erik Swyngedouw

David Harvey is one of the few global public intellectuals whose lifelong political and academic mission is the search for a more genuinely humanizing geography of everyday urban life. His relentless and thought-provoking engagement with the realities and contradictions of contemporary capitalist urbanization has long inspired those seeking to fight for an urban life free from the practices of social, political, and racial exclusion and the divisions that have been the hallmark of modern urbanization throughout the world.

Harvey is one of the urban geographers whose intellectual influence has reached most widely across disciplines. With a Ph.D. in Geography from Cambridge University, he embarked on a lifelong intellectual and political trajectory that has transformed the ways in which urban theorists approach the capitalist city and in which activists seek urban, social, and political change. Already noted for the landmark publication in 1969 of *Explanation in Geography*, his epistemological and political attention soon turned to a more radical and Marxist understanding of the urban. This epistemological shift coincided with his transatlantic migration to the Johns Hopkins University, where he taught Marxist urban theory for the next fifteen years or so. The deep injustices that had just come to the boil in rioting US cities, combined with a rediscovery of the power of historical materialist Marxist analysis, resulted in the publication of *Social Justice and the City* (1973).

Harvey's theorization of the city, deeply embedded in the original writings of Marx, also draws on the radical urban theories and politics pioneered by Henri Lefebvre. For Harvey, cities are—and have always been—highly differentiated spaces of activity, excitement, and pleasure. They are arenas for the pursuit of unoppressed activities and desires, but also ones replete with systematic power, danger, oppression, domination, and exclusion. Exploring the tensions between this dialectical twin of emancipation and disempowerment has been at the centre of Harvey's theoretical and political concerns. Questions of justice cannot be seen independently from the urban condition, not only because most of the world's population now lives in cities, but above all because the city condenses the manifold tensions and contradictions that infuse modern life. These insights were developed fully in Harvey's intellectually most monumental work, *Limits to Capital* (1981), an excavation of the political, economic, and geographical dynamics of capitalism. The book not only brings together the core of Marx's analysis brilliantly but also expands and renews Marxist theory, particularly with respect to the functioning of money and finance and to the 'spatial moment' in the unfolding of capitalist crisis formation. It sets the parameters from which his subsequent engagements with urban theory and practice can be seen.

Harvey went on to explore the interweaving of cultural, social, and political-economic processes in the development of capitalist urbanization in the twin volumes *The Urbanization of Capital* and *Consciousness and the Urban Experience* (1985). His temporary return to the UK to take up the Halford McKinder Chair of Geography at Oxford University was followed by the publication of *The Condition of Postmodernity* (1989), a book intended to be a theoretical and political intervention in what was rapidly becoming a new terrain in urban research. Again from a broadly Marxist perspective, Harvey shows how the condition of postmodernity reflects and embodies the contradictory cultural and political-economic dynamics of capitalism since the 1970s. For him, accelerating time-space compression and the ongoing 'annihilation of space by time' parallels a radical overhaul of the cultural and socio-spatial experiences of space and time and, in so doing, reflects the emergence of a new urban condition. Differentiation and fragmentation at all levels have become the corollary of internationalization, globalization, and the creeping imposition of a total(izing) commodity culture. Growing inter- and intra-regional disparities and the fragmentation, pulverization, and proliferation of bodily, local, regional, and national identities by a homogenizing global cultural landscape of production and consumption have prompted more intense local resistances to the cultural norms increasingly imposed by the tyranny of a spreading 'market-Stalinism' and its accompanying injustices.

In *Justice, Nature, and the Geography of Difference* (1986), Harvey reconsiders urban environmental questions in the context of enduring and pervasive injustices. These questions have become particularly acute as the post-war hope for a more just and redistributional city has been shattered. What has happened instead in the past two decades is that a reinvigorated belief in the powers of the 'hidden hand' of the market to encourage the trickling down of wealth has shifted the ideological terrain. Attempts to foster a collective perspective have given way to celebrations of the virtues of individualism. This market-led urban development has diverted attention away from issues of distribution and socio-economic power. Exclusion and social polarization have come to the fore as the rights of citizens have diminished. In such a context, can one still hope to chart an alternative urban trajectory? Does the clarion call for a more just urbanization inevitably lead to repression and dominance, or is an enabling and empowering urbanization in fact still possible today?

Harvey's answer to these questions is an unqualified 'yes'. The new urbanism is a decidedly pluralist ideal in which the unoppressed expression of desires, dreams, and aspirations can be achieved via a distinct politics of difference that unashamedly captures utopian desires in a progressive and emancipatory fashion, that revels in the 'militant particularisms' of distinct localized identities and struggles for empowerment, but that also aspires to be universalist in its inclusions and global in its connections.

In *Spaces of Hope* (2000), Harvey attempts to imagine alternative urban visions and to chart the contours for a humanized urbanism in the face of the disempowering, uneven development of capitalist forms of urbanization. He shows how the quest for justice in the midst of difference, for empowerment in the face of exclusion, and for pleasurable living is negotiated and enacted in the fractured and fissured spaces of the modern city. These are the spaces of hope that Harvey wishes to bring to our attention. His quest to humanize the city underlies his contribution to this volume and will continue to shape urban thought and politics for a long time to come.

The Right to the City

David Harvey

The city, the noted urban sociologist Robert Park once wrote, is:

Man's most consistent and, on the whole, his most successful attempt to remake the world he lives in more after his heart's desire. But, if the city is the world which man created, it is the world in which he is henceforth condemned to live. Thus, indirectly, and without any clear sense of the nature of his task, in making the city man has remade himself.[1]

The city can be judged and understood only in relation to what I, you, we and, lest we forget, 'they' desire. If the city does not accord with those desires, then it must be changed. The right to the city, says Henri Lefebvre, 'cannot be conceived of as a simple visiting right or as a return to traditional cities'. On the contrary, 'it can only be formulated as a transformed and renewed right to urban life'.[2] The right to the city is, therefore, far more than a right of access to what already exists: it is a right to change it. We must, of course, think carefully about whether we can live with both the intended and unintended consequences of our own creations—a problem every architect and utopian thinker needs to confront. But even more importantly, we need to evaluate continuously what we might be making of ourselves as well as of others as the urban process evolves. If, with experience and on reflection, we find our lives to be too stressful, alienating or just too plain uncomfortable and unrewarding, then we have the right to change course and seek to remake ourselves in another image by constructing a qualitatively different kind of city. The right to make and remake ourselves in this way is, I hold, one of the most precious of all human rights.

But there are many forces that militate against the free exercise of such rights, that even prevent us from thinking and acting in terms of such rights at all. To begin with, the extraordinary pace and scale of urbanization over the last hundred years (which have seen the urban population increase from less than 10 per cent to almost half of the entire world population) has made reflection on this theme difficult. The sheer pace of historical and geographical change overwhelms our capacity to construe, let alone, as Park puts it, to 'clarify' our task. We have, in short, been remade several times over without knowing why, how, or wherefore. Has this contributed to human well-being and happiness, or not? Has it made us into better people, or left us dangling in a world of anomy and alienation, anger and frustration?

We live in divided cities. And, it seems, increasingly so. More and more defensive walls go up as other barriers to movement come down. How we view the world and define possibilities all too often depends which side of the tracks we are on. Perhaps it has always been so. The city has never been a harmonious place, free of confusions, conflicts, and violence. We have only to read the histories of the Paris Commune of 1871, the draft riots of 1864 so brilliantly depicted (though with scant regard for historical accuracy) in Martin Scorcese's film *Gangs of New York* (2002), and think how far we have come. Then we should think too of the urban violence that has more recently consumed Belfast, destroyed Beirut and Sarajevo, rocked Bombay and Ahmedabad, and turned much of the West Bank into rubble. Nor has Los Angeles—that city of angels—been spared. Calmness and civility in urban history are the exception not the rule. The only interesting question is whether outcomes can be creative or destructive. Usually they are both: the city has long been an epicentre of creative destruction.

Globalization (whatever that means) has not changed that one jot. To begin with, so-called 'global' cities are divided socially between the financial elites and the great swathes of lower-paid service workers melding into the marginalized and unemployed. In New York during the boom years of the 1990s, Manhattan median incomes rose at the hefty rate of nearly 12 per cent, but those in the boroughs of Bronx, Queens, Staten Island, and Brooklyn fell between 2 and 4 per cent. The city has always been the site of uneven geographical developments (sometimes of a wholly benevolent and exciting sort), but in certain times and places, the differences proliferate and intensify in negative and even pathological ways that inevitably sow seeds of civil strife. There is another kind of division that needs to be noted. It is fashionable to set aside those cities given over to financial and command functions as if they were the only ones that are truly global. But the global cities of production are just as important and these have names such as Ciudad Juarez, Dacca, Shanghai, Seoul, Taipei, Hong Kong, Jakarta, Ho-Chi-Minh City, Manila, Bombay, and Bangalore, where the global sweatshops and degrading factory systems of a global capitalism grind away to produce my Gap shirts, Nike shoes, mechanical toys, and Sony Walkmans.[3] These are the truly global cities where value is produced and reproduced, albeit under the tutelage of oppressive financial and sometimes outright imperial powers centred in cities (like New York) where the control and command functions of global finance parlay their rentier powers into concentrations of enormous wealth.

Migratory streams from everywhere; business elites in motion; professors and consultants on the wing; diasporas networking across borders (often clandestinely); illegals and *sans papiers*; the dispossessed that sleep in doorways and beg on the street in the midst of the greatest affluence; ethnic and religious cleansings; strange mixings and odd confrontations: these are all part and parcel of our churning urban scene, making questions of citizenship and the rights that inhere therein increasingly difficult to define at the very moment they become even more vital to establish in the face of hostile market forces and increasing state surveillance. On the one hand, such differentiations can generate new and wondrous fusions of the sort we see in musical traditions from New Orleans, Lagos, Johannesburg, and London's East End. From this we can conclude that the right to difference is one of the most precious rights of urban dwellers. But difference can also result in bigotry and divisions, marginalizations and exclusions, sometimes boiling over into violent confrontations.

The right to difference comes at a price. Everywhere we find different notions of rights asserted and pursued. The Communards thought they were right to take back Paris from the bourgeoisie in 1871 in order to reconstruct it according to their hearts' desire. The monarchists who came in to kill them thought they were right to take back the city in the name of God and private property. The Catholics and the Protestants both thought they were right in Belfast as they each sought to cleanse their spaces of any sign of the other's existence. So did Shiv Sena in Bombay (a place they prefer to call Mumbai) when it launched its violent cleansing operation against the Muslims in the name of Maharastri nationalism. Were they all not equally exercising their right to the city? If so, as Marx once famously put it, between such equal rights only force can decide.[4] Is this what the right to the city is all about: to beggar my neighbour or to be beggared in return? This seems a far cry from the pious universalisms of the UN Declaration on Human Rights. Or is it? That is the question.

So what, then, do I do if the cities of the world do not accord with my heart's desire, and if I determine that we are not remaking ourselves in sustainable, emancipatory, or even 'civilized' ways? How, in short, can I exercise my right to the city by changing it? Lefebvre's answer is simple in its essence: through social mobilization and collective political and social struggle.[5] But what do I and others struggle for, and what vision do we construct to guide us? And how can social struggle be waged in such a way as to ensure positive outcomes rather than a descent into endless violence? One thing is clear: we cannot let fear of the latter lead us into cowering and mindless passivity. Conflict avoidance is no answer: to slide back into that is to disengage with what urbanization is all about and thereby lose any prospect of exercising any right to the city whatsoever.

There is an interesting parallel between Park's argument and Marx's formulations. We can change ourselves only by changing our world and vice versa, says Marx. That dialectical relation lies at the root of what all human labour is about. There is a crucial role here, says Marx, for imagination and desire. What separates the worst of architects from the best of bees is that the architect erects a structure in the imagination before materializing it upon the ground.[6] It is the metaphor rather than to the profession of the architect to which he appeals. The implication is that we individually and collectively make the city through our daily actions and our political, intellectual, and economic engagements. All of us are, in some way or other, architects of our urban futures. The right to change the city is not an abstract right, but a right that inheres in daily practices, whether we are conscious of that right or not. This is a profound point and the pivot upon which much of my argument turns.

But, conversely—and this is where the dialectic returns to haunt us—the city makes us under urban circumstances that are not of our own choosing. How can I hope for an alternative possible urban world, even imagine its contours, its conundrums, and its charms, when I am so deeply immersed in the experience of what already exists? Can I live in Los Angeles without becoming such a frustrated motorist that I vote endlessly for bond issues to build more and more superhighways? In opening the door to the human imagination, Marx, though he often sought to deny it, creates a utopian moment in which our imaginations can wander and wonder about alternative possible urban worlds. 'Who is not a utopian today?' asks Lefebvre. Can we afford not to be utopian? Can consideration of the utopian tradition reveal a visionary path to inform our perspectives on possibilities and to rally social movements to some alternative and different vision of the city? One without superhighways, for example.

Most of the projects and plans we designate as 'utopian' are fixed and formal designs. They are what I call 'utopias of spatial form': the planned cities and communities that have through the ages beguiled us into thinking that history may stop, that harmony will be established, that human desires will once and for all be fully satiated if not happily realized.[7] But history and change cannot be erased by superimposing a spatial form that locks down all desire for novelty and difference. All such utopias of spatial form end up being repressive of human desire. And, to the degree that they have been implemented, the results have been far more authoritarian and repressive than emancipatory. Why, then, do we still hanker after such utopias, and in what ways can this tradition be mobilized to a more open purpose? Louis Marin here provides an interesting gloss. Utopias of spatial form amount, he suggests, to a form of 'spatial play'.[8] From this perspective we see the immense variety of spatial forms incorporated into different utopian plans as experimental suggestions as to how we might reshape urban spaces more to our heart's desire or, more cogently, to realize a certain social aim, such as greater gender equality, ecological sustainability, cultural diversity, or whatever. Conversely, we also learn to see many of the existing spaces of the city as potential sites, dubbed 'heterotopic' by Lefebvre as well as by Foucault,[9] which can provide socio-spatial bases within which experiments into different modes of urban living can arise and from which struggles can be waged to build a different kind of city.

There is, however, a marked contrast between this spatial specification of urban alternatives and what I call utopias of the social process. In this latter case, we presume that some social process will lead to the promised land. In recent times, for example, neo-liberal theorists (building on the liberal tradition that goes back to John Locke and Adam Smith) have sought to persuade us that freedoms of the market will bring us all wealth, security, and happiness. Against that are set a whole range of radical and revolutionary thinkers who have claimed that social or class struggle will eventually lead us to the perfections of communism, socialism, anarchism, feminism, ecologism, or whatever. Such utopian schemes of social process seem fatally flawed both in theory and in practice. In part, it is that such schemas are abstractly removed from the concrete problems that arise when spatial structures are created on the ground. The territoriality of political power and organization is viewed as neutral in human affairs when we know that, in practice, spatial forms are constitutive of social relations. Such structures of thought ignore what happens when walls, bridges, and doors become frameworks for social action and bases for discriminations. If utopias of spatial form are found wanting because they seek to suppress the force of historical change, then utopias of the social process are equally at fault, because they deny the constitutive significance of spatial organization. Why can we not devise a utopianism of spatio-temporal process, a dialectical utopianism that combines the idea of radical changes in both space and time to fashion an entirely different imagination of what city life could be about?[10]

Even if we could rise to such an intellectual and political challenge, we would still face the difficulty of specifying some idea of what we might be aiming for. Should we follow Lefebvre and seek to fashion ourselves into a non-gendered version of 'a polyvalent, polysensorial, urban man capable of complex and transparent relations with the world (the environment and himself)'?[11] What ethical and moral principles regulating social relations might we seek to embed within such a dialectical utopianism? And by what criteria would we proceed to judge the superiority of this or that path to the definition of some grander set of rights to the city? Would it be reasonable to assert that the quest for social justice ought to be central to our endeavours, as many within the contemporary global justice movement now assert? Can social injustice—as signalled by the ghastly poverty that haunts the world more generally but which is most concentrated in cities—be eradicated, as the World Bank and the

International Monetary Fund insist, by the proper application of some version of free market capitalism?[12]

What is social justice? Thrasymachus in Plato's *Republic* argues that 'each form of government enacts the laws with a view to its own advantage', so that 'the just is the same everywhere, the advantage of the stronger'. Plato rejects this cynical view in favour of justice as a specifiable ideal.[13] A plethora of ideal formulations now exist from which we can choose. We could be egalitarian; utilitarian in the manner of Bentham (the greatest good of the greatest number); contractual in the manner of Rousseau (with his ideal of inalienable rights) or John Rawls; cosmopolitan in the manner of Kant (a wrong to one is a wrong to all); or just plain Hobbesian, insisting that the state (Leviathan) impose justice upon reckless private interests to prevent social life being nasty, brutish, and short. Some writers, disturbed by the deracinated universalism of such theories of justice, even argue for local ideals of justice that are sensitive to cultural and geographical differences.[14] We stare frustrated in the mirror, asking: 'Mirror, mirror, on the wall, which is the most just theory of justice of them all?' We worry that Thrasymachus might have been right and that justice is simply whatever the ruling class wants it to be. And when we look at the history of jurisprudence, of judicial decisions, and of how these have evolved in relation to political power, it is very hard to deny that ideals of justice and practices of political power have marched along hand in hand. Foucault, for one, has plausibly questioned again and again the class neutrality of any discourse on rights, let alone of any system of adjudication through the courts.[15]

Yet we cannot do without the concept of justice for the simple reason that the sense of injustice has historically been one of the most potent seedbeds of all to animate the quest for social change. The idea of justice, in alliance with notions of rights, has been not only a powerful provocateur in political movements but the object of an immense effort of articulation. The challenge is, therefore, not to relativize ideals of social justice and of rights, but to contextualize them. When we do that, we see that certain dominant social processes throw up and rest upon certain conceptions of rights and of social justice. To challenge those particular rights is to challenge the social process in which they inhere. Conversely, it is impossible to wean society away from one dominant social process (such as that of capital accumulation through market exchange) to another (such as political democracy and collective action) without simultaneously shifting allegiance from one dominant conception of rights and of social justice to another.

The difficulty with all idealist specifications of rights and of justice is that they hide this connection. Only when they are concretely related to some social process do they find social meaning. This problem is apparent in John Rawls's theory of justice as fairness.[16] He seeks a neutral standpoint from which to specify a universal conception of justice. He constructs a 'veil of ignorance' around the position we might occupy in the social order and asks how we would specify a just distribution in the light of that ignorance. The trouble is that he cannot presume total ignorance since nothing whatsoever could then be said. He therefore assumes that we know the general laws of human psychology and of economic behaviour and that we are familiar with the dominant processes through which the social order is reproduced. But these are not universal truths. In what historical time and geographical place do I locate myself? To what school of economic or psychological thought do I attach myself? If I can choose between classical political economy, marginalist economics (with its thesis that fairness is given by the marginal rates of return on scarcity of land, labour, and capital), or some version of deep ecology or Marxian or feminist theory, then the outcomes will plainly be quite different. Hardly surprisingly, Rawls's system ends up largely confirming notions of rights inherent in the market and in bourgeois society, even as it concedes that there is no real way to adjudicate between socialist and capitalist ways of doing things.

We therefore need to shift attention away from consideration of abstract universals towards the relation of concepts of rights and of justice to social processes. Consider, for example, the dominant social processes at work within our own world. They cluster around two dominant logics of power: that of the territorial state, and that of capital.[17] These two logics of power are often in tension, if not outright opposition to each other, at the same time as they must in some way fulfil and support each other lest social reproduction dissolve into total anarchy and nihilism.

Consider, first, the territorial logic of state powers. However much we might wish rights to be universal, as the UN Declaration of Universal Rights (1948) first envisaged, it requires the protection of the state apparatus to enforce those rights. Much of the work of Amnesty International has been to call upon states to acknowledge and live up to their responsibilities in this regard. But if political power is not willing to do so, then rights remain empty shells. Rights in this instance are fundamentally derivative of, and conditional upon, citizenship and territorialized power (primarily but not uniquely expressed as state power). The territoriality of jurisdiction then becomes an issue. This cuts both ways. Difficult questions now arise because of stateless persons, migrants without papers, illegal immigrants, and the like. Who is or is not a 'citizen' becomes a serious issue defining principles of inclusion and exclusion within the territorial specification of the national or local state (in which jurisdiction, for example, can I cast my vote?). How the state exercises sovereignty is itself a huge issue and, as has been asserted in numerous writings in recent years, there are limits placed on that sovereignty (even at the national as well as at the local level) by the rules that govern the circulation and accumulation of capital across the globe. Nevertheless, the nation state, with its monopoly over legitimate forms of violence, can in Hobbesian fashion define its own bundle of rights and its own interpretations of them and be only loosely bound by international conventions. Even the United States insists on its right not to be held accountable for crimes against humanity as defined in the international arena at the same time as it insists that war criminals from elsewhere must be brought to justice before the very same courts whose authority it denies in relation to its own citizens.

The right to the city is therefore mediated by the spatial organization of political powers. Patterns of urban administration, policing, and regulation are all embedded in a system of governance that allows for the playing out of multiple interests in the murky corridors of urban politics and through the labyrinthine channels of urban bureaucracy and administration. Certain rights are coded within these systems. But others are simply denied or, more likely, rendered so opaque by bureaucratic fudging as to be meaningless. Planning powers (where this zone is designated for commerce, and that one condemned for insalubrity), edicts to regulate behaviour ('no loitering here'), surveillance (video cameras on every corner), lopsided service provision (clean streets here, garbage dumps there), and the desperate attempt to impose order, suppress crime and conflict, and bring regularity to daily life in the city: these are everywhere in evidence. Urban citizenship (the rights of immigrants, transients, and strangers to participate in local politics) is an even murkier concept than that of the state, since it so often depends on residence and domicile in a social world that is now more than ever constructed on principles of motion. State powers are invariably obsessed with maintaining order and erasing difference when both disorder and difference are fundamental to the creativity of urban life. It is all too often only through struggle against the dead weight of state and territorialized power that a different right to the city can be asserted. In many a city, the homeless find that struggle to be at the very core of their everyday lives. To them, the injustice is palpable while, to the rest of society, they are simply categorized as a public nuisance and administered their just deserts accordingly.[18] While the rights in this case may theoretically be opposed but equal, the force exercised to determine outcomes is invariably lopsided.

The capitalistic logic of power, on the other hand, rests upon a quite different conception of rights, based in private property and individual ownership. To live in a capitalist society is to accept or submit to the bundle of rights necessary if capital accumulation and market exchange are to proceed in a legally justifiable and enforceable way. These are the rights codified in universal language in the UN Declaration of 1948. The state is supposed to act as guarantor of those rights. Though it sometimes signally fails to support them, the state needs money to maintain and enhance its power and is therefore very much, in contemporary times, at the mercy of the capitalistic logic of power (even when state influence is not bought outright, in many instances quite legally, through the corruptions of money power).

We live, therefore, in a society in which the inalienable rights of individuals to private property and the profit rate trump any other conception of inalienable rights you can think of. Defenders of this regime of rights plausibly argue that it encourages 'bourgeois virtues' without which everyone in the world would be far worse off. These include personal and individual responsibility, independence from state interference (which often places this regime of rights in severe opposition to those defined by the state), equality of opportunity in the market and before the law, rewards for initiative and entrepreneurial endeavours, care for oneself and one's own, and an open market place that allows for wide-ranging freedoms of choice of both contract and exchange. This system of rights appears even more persuasive when extended to the right of private property in one's own body (which underpins the right of the individual freely to sell his or her labour power as well as to be treated with dignity and respect and to be free from bodily coercions such as slavery) and the right to freedom of thought, expression, and speech. These derivative rights are appealing. Many of us rely heavily upon them. But we do so much as beggars live off the crumbs from the rich man's table.

There is no way I can convince anyone by philosophical argument that the capitalistic regime of rights is unjust. It might, of course, be willingly conceded by proponents that this system of rights is imperfect and not without contradictions, and that things may certainly go wrong with respect to actual application, particularly since incompatibility with state requirements is often identifiable and the collective rights of minorities to cultural difference are hard to protect given the individualism presupposed within the prevailing system. Lacking any plausible alternative, these contradictions and faults of application can be worked out, the argument goes, given common sense and goodwill on the part of conflicting interests within society.

My objection to this regime of rights is quite simple: to accept it is to accept that we have no alternative except to live under a regime of endless capital accumulation and economic growth, no matter what the social, ecological, or political consequences. It also implies that this endless capital accumulation must be geographically expanded by extension of such rights across the globe. This is exactly what globalization and its institutional framework, embodied by the World Trade Organization, the IMF, and the World Bank are about. Imperialism of some sort is inevitable.[19] Consider a recent example of such reasoning. Claiming that the 9/11 tragedy of 2001 had clarified America's role in the world and opened up great opportunities, President Bush, in an op-ed piece for the *New York Times* on the anniversary of that tragedy and in a statement that closely followed the prologue to the US National Defence Strategy issued shortly thereafter, asserted: 'We will use our position of unparalleled strength and influence to build an atmosphere of international order and openness in which progress and liberty can flourish in many nations. A peaceful world of growing freedom serves American long-term interests, reflects enduring American ideals and unites America's allies.' We seek, he wrote, as he prepared to go to war, 'a just peace where repression, resentment, and poverty are replaced with the hope of democracy, development, free markets, and free trade', these last two having 'proved their ability to lift whole societies out of poverty'. The United States will deliver this gift of freedom (of the market) to the world whether it likes it or not.[20] The inalienable rights of private property and the profit rate will be universally established. These are the rights that are depicted as standing for goodness in a sea of evil.

But the effects of such rights—on our life chances, our cities, our security, and prospects—are not necessarily benign. Free markets are not necessarily fair. 'There is', the old saying goes, 'nothing more unequal than the equal treatment of unequals.' This is how the market works. It is, on the one hand, very egalitarian. But it also operates, when uncontrolled, to ensure that the rich grow richer and the poor poorer through the egalitarianism of market exchange. Free markets cannot produce fairness when initial endowments are unequal, when monopoly power is exercised, and when the institutional frameworks of exchange are affected, as they always are, by asymmetries in power relations. 'In the name of the free market system,' reports Seabrook, Indonesia 'promotes the grossest violations of human rights, and undermines the right to subsist of those on whose labour its competitive advantage rests.'[21] The liberalization not only of trade but of financial markets across the globe has unleashed a storm of speculative powers in which predatory capital has plundered the world to the detriment of all else. A few hedge funds, exercising their right to make a profit and protected by the legal fiction that the corporation is in effect a private person, can move around the world speculatively destroying whole economies (such as those of Indonesia and Thailand). They destroy our cities with their speculations and then reanimate them with their donations to the opera and the ballet while their CEOs strut the global stage accumulating massive wealth at the expense of millions of people. No wonder those of wealth and power support such rights while seeking to persuade us of their universality and goodness.

Unregulated free market capitalism widens class divisions,

exacerbates social inequality, and ensures that rich regions grow richer while the rest plunge deeper and deeper into the mire of poverty. Cities then become more ghettoized as the rich seal themselves off for protection. And if racial, religious, and ethnic divisions crosscut, as they so often do, with struggles to acquire class and income position, then we quickly find cities divided in the bitter ways we know only too well. Furthermore, free market competition typically results in monopoly or oligopoly power. Thirty years of neo-liberalism have brought us immense concentrations of corporate power in energy, the media, pharmaceuticals, transportation, and even retailing (look at Wal-Mart). The freedom of the market that Bush proclaims as the high point of human aspiration towards individual liberty turns out to be nothing more than the convenient means to spread corporate monopoly power and Coca Cola everywhere without constraint.

Worse still, markets require scarcity for them to function. If scarcity does not exist, then it must be socially created. This is what private property and the profit rate do. Enclosure of the commons and the destruction of common property rights through the privatization and commodification of all things are necessary preconditions for capital accumulation to proceed. Education, healthcare, water, and sanitation have to be privatized and brought within the dominant regime of rights favourable to the circulation and accumulation of capital. What I call 'accumulation by dispossession' becomes a dominant motif.[22] One of the key elements in this is the loss of any sense of collective rights to the city and their displacement by individualized rights of capital accumulation and private property through urban development. The city is turned over to the growth machines, the financiers, the developers, the speculators, and the profiteers. The result is unnecessary deprivation (unemployment, housing shortages, and so on) in the midst of plenty. Hence the homeless on our streets and the beggars in the subways. Famines occur in the midst of food surpluses. Basic needs, such as clean water, are denied to those who do not have the ability to pay. The excluded are forced to drink from cholera-infested rivers. This is what free markets actually do, and this is what attachment to the inalienable rights of private property and of the profit rate really means, no matter what are the pious assertions emanating from the main centres of capitalist power. Even the World Bank admits that poverty, both absolute and relative, has grown rather than diminished during the halcyon days of neo-liberalism on the world stage.[23] But it then insists that it is only through the propagation of neo-liberal rights of private property and the profit rate in the market place that poverty can be eliminated!

If this is where the inalienable rights of private property and the profit rate lead, then I want none of it. I am not alone in that conclusion. There is a huge movement for global justice that clearly sees the nature of the problem even as it struggles to identify viable alternatives. This bundle of rights and the social process in which it is embedded produce cities marked and marred by inequality, alienation, and injustice. In response, urban social movements arise that oppose the endless accumulation of capital and its associated conception of rights. A different right to the city must be asserted; a different version of the urban process must be constructed.

Those that now have the rights will not surrender them willingly. Remember: 'between equal rights, force decides'. This does not necessarily mean violence (though, sadly, it often comes down to that). But it does mean the mobilization of sufficient power through political organization as well as in the streets to change things. But by what strategies do we proceed? Can the territoriality of political power be used against this bourgeois regime of rights? In 'Red Bologna' in the 1970s, and in contemporary Port Alegre in southern Brazil (the city that has hosted the World Social Forum these last three years), the presumed answer to this question has been 'yes'.[24] Political and urban social movements have used the city as an agent of social and political innovation in the search to construct an alternative social order and a different sense of the right to the city. Can the city be a centre of revolution? It has often been so in the past. Can it be so again?

No social order, said Saint-Simon, can change without the lineaments of the new already being latently present within the existing state of things.[25] Revolutions are not total breaks; what they do is turn things upside down. Derivative rights (like the right to be treated with dignity) should become fundamental and fundamental rights (of private property and the profit rate) should become derivative. Was this not the traditional aim of democratic socialism as it sought, with some success, to use the territoriality of political power to regulate and tame the rights of capital?

There are, it also turns out, contradictions within the capitalist package of rights that can be exploited for political gain. What would have happened to global capitalism and urban life had the UN Declaration's clauses on the derivative rights of labour (to a secure job, reasonable living standards, and the right to organize) been rigorously enforced? But new rights can also be defined, such as the right to the city, which, as I began by saying, is not merely a right of access to what the property speculators and state planners define, but an active right to make the city more in accord with our hearts' desire, and to remake ourselves thereby in a different image.

Such shifts in perspectives mean little if they remain a purely individual affair. They demand a collective effort. The right to the city cannot be construed simply as an individualized right. It must be understood as a collective right and its exercise depends crucially upon the shaping of a collective politics. The creation of a new urban commons, a public sphere of active democratic participation, requires that we roll back that huge wave of privatization that has been the mantra of a destructive neo-liberalism in the last few years. We must imagine a more inclusive city, even if it is a continuously fractious one, based not only upon a different ordering of rights but upon different political and economic practices. Individualized rights to be treated with dignity as a human being and to freedoms of expression are too precious to be set aside, but to these we must add the right to adequate life chances for all, to elementary material supports, to inclusion, and to difference. The right to the city, as I began by saying, is not merely a conditional right of access to what already exists; it is an active right to make the city different, to shape it more in accord with our collective needs and desires, and so to remake our daily lives, reshape our architectural practices, and define an alternative way of simply being human.

But it is here that the conception of the right to the city takes on another gloss. It was in the streets that the Czechs liberated themselves from oppressive forms of governance in 1989, and in Tiananmen Square that the Chinese student movement sought to establish an alternative definition of rights; it was through massive street demonstrations that the Vietnam War was pushed to closure, and it was in the streets that millions protested against the prospect of US imperialist intervention in Iraq on 15 February 2003. The streets of Seattle, Genoa, Melbourne, Quebec City, and Bangkok are where the inalienable rights of private property and of the profit rate have been challenged. As Mitchell says:

If the right to the city is a cry and a demand, then it is only a cry that is heard and a demand that has force to the degree that there is a space from and within which this cry and demand is visible. In public space—on street corners or in parks, in the streets during riots and demonstrations—political organizations can represent themselves to a larger population, and through this representation give their cries and their demands some force. By claiming space in public, by creating public spaces, social groups themselves become public.[26]

The inalienable right to the city rests upon the capacity to force open spaces of the city to protest and contention, to create unmediated public spaces so that the cauldron of urban life can become a catalytic site from which new conceptions and configurations of urban living can be devised, and out of which new and less damaging conceptions of rights can be constructed. The right to the city is not a gift. It has to be seized by political movement.

If our urban world has been imagined and made, then it can be reimagined and remade. The task may be difficult. Bertolt Brecht had it right when he wrote:

It takes a lot of things to change the world:
Anger and tenacity, science and indignation,
The quick initiative, the long reflection,
The cold patience and the infinite perseverance,
The understanding of the particular case and the understanding of
  the ensemble,
Only the lessons of reality can teach us to transform reality.[27]

The inalienable right to the city is worth fighting for. 'City air makes one free', it used to be said. The air is a bit polluted now. But it can always be cleaned up.

4

Introduction to
James D. Wolfensohn

Sebastian Mallaby

James David Wolfensohn is a surprising figure. A wildly successful investment banker, he nonetheless found time to take up the cello in middle life; he would cross the Atlantic on Concorde, buying two seats so that his cello could fly with him. A corporate insider, he nonetheless identified with the world's least fortunate; he took an interest in international family planning, the environment, and AIDS, even as he was merging and restructuring the world's leading companies. Appointed to lead a World Bank known chiefly for prescribing macro-economic austerity, Wolfensohn distanced the institution from both macro-economics and prescriptions. He spoke the language of poverty-fighting groups such as Oxfam, and demanded social justice; and after his first press conference, the World Bank's chief spin doctor, who was concerned that the Bank not be seen as 'soft', remarked that Wolfensohn had not been 'on message'. 'He's the President,' another official said. 'I think you'll find that *is* the message.'

Since that exchange in 1995, Wolfensohn has reshaped the Bank, a formidable, sprawling institution with nearly ten thousand employees and projects in about one hundred countries. The emphasis on macro-economic structural adjustment, which had dominated the Bank's programmes since the start of the 1980s, was phased out; questions of governance—the transparency of political institutions, the level of corruption, the quality of judicial or media or civil society oversight—came to preoccupy the Bank almost as much as price signals and sound budgeting. Before Wolfensohn's arrival, the Bank's apolitical charter was thought to put these governance issues at least partially off limits. But in a speech in 1996, Wolfensohn denounced 'the cancer of corruption', and a taboo that had lasted since the Bank's creation in 1944 was abruptly shattered.

Wolfensohn's focus on poverty and social justice come through strongly in his contribution to this volume. Before his arrival at the Bank, the institution was often vilified for technocratic elitism: its officials' idea of 'field work' was a meeting with a finance minister in a five-star hotel, according to the critics. But in this lecture we find Wolfensohn recounting the life of a poor mother in a Brazilian slum, and explaining that the worst feature of poverty is 'voicelessness'. This rhetorical focus on individuals—an attempt, as Wolfensohn himself expresses it, to put a 'human face' on development—has been a hallmark of his leadership. It has helped to carry the Bank through a crisis in its popular legitimacy in 1999–2001, the high point of the anti-globalization protests.

Wolfensohn's preoccupation with governance issues such as corruption comes through just as powerfully in this volume. The Bank started out in the 1940s as a financier of infrastructure, and right up into the 1980s it would have described its chief role in urban development in terms of water systems, roads, and electricity. But in this lecture and in much of his speaking, Wolfensohn offers a different emphasis. The Bank's contribution, in his view, is to promote strong political institutions to oversee urban renewal: he is more interested in training mayors than in laying concrete. Years of experience have taught that there is no point drilling water holes if they are not subsequently maintained, or if corruption distorts access to them. Hence Wolfensohn's stress on the quality of urban leadership.

This emphasis on governance, like previous phases in the history of the Bank, reflects shifting patterns of thinking among development economists. The concrete-pouring focus of the Bank's early period was underpinned by the conventional wisdom of the time, which held that the chief bottleneck to growth was a simple lack of capital; if you could address that 'savings gap' by building power stations or roads, then poverty would be defeated. In the 1960s and 1970s, this thinking was replaced: education and training were now regarded as the key to development, and so the Bank branched out from physical to human capital. In the 1980s, the new wisdom was that neither infrastructure nor health nor education was enough: no economy could take off unless budgets balanced, inflation was checked, and firms faced real price signals. By the mid-1990s, however, fifteen years of experiment with pro-market prescriptions had produced disappointing results, largely because the prescriptions were seldom implemented consistently. The Bank therefore moved on to the next theory: to make good economic policy stick, poor countries need healthy politics.

If this conviction lies behind Wolfensohn's stress on the quality of mayors, an allied insight explains his enthusiasm for 'South–South contacts'—for the idea of linking developing country urban leaders to one another via the internet. In its macro-economic phase, the Bank learned that its prescriptions were usually ignored; there was no point preaching change from Washington; domestic political will, not external pressure, is the key to good policy. To build that political will, the Bank increasingly seeks to convey knowledge rather than handing down prescriptions; if it wants to persuade a municipality to reform water tariffs, it will encourage city officials to study the experience of similar reforms in other cities in their region. Wolfensohn's enthusiasm for internet knowledge-sharing in this lecture is part of this new drive. He has forged a humbler Bank: a partner and adviser to poor governments rather than an overseer.

Wolfensohn is considerably less deferential, however, when addressing European or American audiences. From his first months at the Bank, he has striven to shake comfortable audiences awake: to insist that the cause of development is both morally urgent and vital to the rich world's interests. In this volume, Wolfensohn reminds us of the scale of global poverty, something he does in almost every speech he gives, and he adds an urban slant: in 1950, New York City was the only metropolis with a population of over 10 million people; by 2015, there will be twenty-one such megalopolises, seventeen of which will be in developing countries; if we are concerned with the problems of cities, we must focus our thinking on the challenges faced by poor countries. As Wolfensohn tells us, 56 per cent of the urban population of Africa currently live in slums. In Asia the figure is 37 per cent, and in Latin America it is no less than 76 per cent.

The moral part of Wolfensohn's argument is surely beyond doubt. We live in a world in which one part of humanity enjoys 2-dollar coffees and disposable cameras, while another part lives on 2 dollars a day and appears itself to be disposable. But the security part of Wolfensohn's argument is debatable, and whether or not you think that the slums of São Paolo threaten the security of Toulouse, history suggests that the public consensus in support of this proposal is likely to be fleeting. Over the past sixty years, we have passed through phases when security has galvanized the rich world's efforts to address international poverty. Think of the end of the 1940s, when the connection between the 1930s depression and the rise of Fascism was too obvious to ignore, or think of the Cold War neurosis following the Cuban revolution of 1959, which led to a sharp expansion in the World Bank's resources and of foreign aid more generally. The attacks of 11 September 2001, to which Wolfensohn refers in this lecture, have created another such moment. With luck it will be used to re-energize the struggle against poverty. There could be no better memorial to terrorism's victims.

The Undivided City

James D. Wolfensohn

The division between rich and poor that fractured our cities for so long must become a thing of the past. It is the task of the World Bank and of all those engaged in the fight against urban poverty to promote this vision of the city and to make it a reality for urban dwellers all over the world. Nowhere is the task more urgent than in the cities of the developing world where increasing numbers of the poorest citizens live in slums. So I intend, in what follows, to shift the focus of these Lectures on to the developing world and the plight of its slum dwellers. I shall start by offering a general overview of the problem of poverty in the developing world and what is being done to tackle it. I shall then address a particularly acute example of this general problem—urban poverty—and describe the initiative that the World Bank and its partners are taking to meet the challenge of cities without slums. I hope, in so doing, to explain why this initiative is so important, not just for the slum dwellers themselves, but also for us all. It is because the division between rich and poor has no place in the cities of tomorrow. We live in one undivided city.

The Fight against Poverty

The World Bank, created in the aftermath of World War II, was designed initially to oversee the reconstruction and development of those countries devastated by the war. Over the last sixty years or so, it has developed into an institution whose central task is to fight poverty throughout the world. We at the World Bank perform this task in the belief that the reduction of poverty is a necessary precursor to the promotion of equity, or fairness for all. If the world is to reduce the huge degree of inequity that exists between peoples and nations today then the first problem to be addressed is that of poverty. It is quite clear where we need to direct our main energies in the fight against poverty. There are 6 billion people on our planet today and 5 billion of them are residents of developing countries. Three billion people live on under 2 US dollars a day, and 1 billion 2 hundred million people on less than 1 US dollar a day. So the particular challenge that faces the World Bank is to address the problem of poverty in the developing world. No one should forget that the dimensions of this problem are, for demographic reasons, expanding at an alarming rate. In the next twenty-five years, the population of our planet is set to grow from 6 to 8 billion, and, since all of that growth will occur in developing countries, the world in 2025 will be one in which 7 billion of its 8 billion inhabitants live in developing countries. What is more, this growth is set to occur entirely in urban populations. The cities of the developing world, in other words, are set to become the frontline in the fight against poverty.

Poverty, people are starting to recognize, is a problem that affects us all. The remarkable election of President Lula in Brazil at the beginning of 2003 seems to have been indicative of a change of mood, a new recognition that has dawned not only in South America but also around the world. President Lula's key campaign messages dwelt on the need for poverty to be tackled head on to build a social system that was equitable for all Brazilians. Several other countries have recently elected presidents and leaders on the promise of similar messages. The feeling is that the growth of social inequity has gone too far and that the problem of poverty must now be addressed. This change of mood has not occurred because, all of a sudden, people have become more altruistic, but because they have recognized that, in a globalized world, what happens in one place inevitably affects people in another. That is, indeed, precisely what 'globalization' means: the fact that, in the areas of health, education, communications, finance, migration, and so many others, we all belong, for better or for worse, to one world. No event can have brought that notion home more forcibly, to the American people at least, than the terrorist attacks of 11 September 2001: the collapse of the World Trade Center, the attack on the Pentagon, and the crash at a field in Pennsylvania. For these attacks showed that what happens in some distant and desperately poor country, like Afghanistan, have direct consequences from which none of us can escape. Many people, not just in the United States but also throughout the world, came to the view, as a result of the September 11 attacks, that poverty is not just an issue of ethics or charity but one of direct self-interest. All of us, in our globalized world, are subject to the consequences of poverty wherever it exists. Poverty in one place is poverty everywhere. This was true, of course, long before the events of September 11 brought it home to many in the developed world. Fighting poverty, as I have already said, has been the aim of the World Bank for decades. It is also enshrined in the Millennium Development Goals, a set of initiatives designed to make the world a better place, which were adopted by the entire United Nations membership in the year 2000.[1] One of these Goals, which are to be achieved by 2015, is a key commitment to halve poverty worldwide. This commitment includes a target specifically related to urban poverty to which I shall return later. For now, though, I refer to the Millennium Development Goals simply as a further indication of the recent sea change in world opinion. National leaders, as well as those they represent, have recognized that the world must unite its forces in the fight to reduce poverty.

But how is the goal of poverty reduction to be achieved? We at the World Bank decided that we could answer that question only once we understood exactly what poverty was. The people best qualified to tell us were clearly the poor themselves. So we undertook an extensive study, entitled *Voices of the Poor*, in which we interviewed some 60 thousand of the rural and urban poor in sixty countries in order to hear from them at first hand about the experience of poverty.[2] This study produced insights that now essentially determine the central objectives and approach of the World Bank in this key area of its activities. For what poor people say about their situation is deeply interesting. They do not start by talking about a lack of money. They talk instead of the need for their voices to be heard, of the need for recognition, freedom from fear, opportunity, and an end to hunger. The women, in particular, aspire towards freedom from fear and from gender persecution. All ask, not for charity, but for an opportunity to make something of their lives. What people in slums, shanties, and villages of the developing world want above all is the chance to work towards the betterment of themselves and their children. The term 'developing world' is not a politically correct euphemism: it expresses the fundamental desire of the vast numbers of people to whom it refers. These are not strange people from another planet; they are like us, and their desires are the same as ours. Of course they are looking for additional funding, for they know what a difference that funding will make, but they want to earn it for themselves. Paying heed to the voices of the poor means above all attempting to give them the place in society which is so often denied them.

Poverty reduction, as the world's poorest people have told us, starts in social inclusion, a culture of partnership, and a sense of ownership. Take the example of Maria Vargas, just one of the many people interviewed as part of the *Voices of the Poor* study.[3] Maria migrated as a young woman from Alagoas in rural Brazil to Sacadura Cabral in an attempt to escape poverty. Sacadura Cabral is a *favela*, an urban slum where many homes lack legal tenure, close to the centre of Brazil's largest and most industrialized city, São Paolo. Sacadura Cabral used to offer its 3 thousand or so migrant settlers plenty of work in heavy industry. But it has suffered severe job losses in the last decade, the unpaved streets run with rain-water and sewage, and crime is rife in the area. Maria's experience is typical of that described by many poor people who contributed to the *Voices of the Poor* study in Brazil. Like Maria, many women have become the only breadwinners in their households, and are forced daily to fight for survival in an increasingly violent urban world. Maria has seen the worst of this world, notably in the rape and murder of her 4-year-old daughter, of whom she says:

If she were alive she would be 18 and beautiful. I suffered a lot with this; the whole family suffered. My eldest son withdrew from school for some time. The teachers kept calling me about it. He was the one who found her in that condition. I was not at home when she disappeared. I spent six days looking for her.

Maria has a partner, but refuses to live with him, wishing to avoid problems between him and her children. Surrounded by poverty and violence, she has nevertheless managed, against all the odds, to give her sons a start in life. The key to social inclusion, she and many others in her position believe, is education. She never allowed any of her sons to give up school, even when they had to repeat courses, and today all are earning a living and studying to win places at university. 'I raised all my children amid drugs, robbery, cocaine, marijuana, and crack, but thanks to God none of them ever got involved with these things,' says Maria. 'For a poor mother living in a *favela* with many sons, it is a victory.'

Identifying social inclusion, a culture of partnership, and a sense of ownership as the crucial elements in poverty reduction is one thing. But making these things a reality for poor people is quite another. Actions to help achieve this need not be expensive to implement, but do require significant quantities of leadership, vision, and political will. This challenge has led us to adopt an entirely new paradigm of development. Gone are the days when an international institution such as the World Bank worked alone, simply handing out money to a national government. The development paradigm has evolved from singular initiatives to a coordinated approach: those of us who are used to doing our own thing must now be prepared to enter into a dialogue. The idea is to foster a partnership led by the citizens of developing countries that best reflects their interests: a coalition of forces that include international institutions such as the Bank and bilateral institutions such as the Department for International Development (DfID) in the UK, but also civil society, the private sector, and poor people themselves exercising their rights as full citizens. One of my current tasks is to convince the World Bank Board of Governors that there should be a dialogue between development institutions and the faiths. This dialogue, which would have been out of the question in the past, is absolutely essential in the case of Africa, for example, where 50 per cent of education and health provision is delivered by faith-based organizations. They too have a place in the new partnerships. The debate around development today is not about whether, but simply about how we bring all these partners together to deal with questions of poverty; how we define the priorities, measure the results obtained, and meet appropriate demands for effectiveness and success. Countries need to decide what they realistically expect and hope will be done—not by tomorrow, because these issues cannot be solved in a day, a month, or even a year—but over a period of ten or fifteen years. This is the new challenge that world leaders have set us all in the Millennium Development Goals of 2015.

I want to finish this overview by touching briefly on a final point, namely, that what I have been saying about countries in general applies directly to cities. There is no difference made between rural and urban dwellers, or between urban dwellers and the rest of a country's population, in the new development paradigm. What we have found in broad terms is that, if the people of a country are to become better off, they need good government, fair regulations, impartial and effective administrations, a legal and judicial framework that protects their rights, financial systems that work, and a civil society that is free from corruption. Beyond these conditions, they need a decent education system, healthcare, infrastructure, and access to secure tenure. These necessary conditions cannot be imposed upon a country by the *fiat* of a monolithic development paradigm. For each country has its own history, culture, and social fabric, and any effective strategy for reform must therefore be grounded in these realities. Development works best, in short, when people in the countries affected themselves take the lead in the fight against the poverty and the social division from which they suffer. The same, as we shall see, is true in the cities.

Cities without Slums

What then, within this broad picture, has been happening in the cities of the developing world? When I first started working at the World Bank, the emphasis was on the elimination of poverty in rural areas. The statistics give the lie to that emphasis. For the world is continuing to urbanize rapidly—and particularly in developing countries. In 1900, 233 million people, 14 per cent of the world's population, lived in towns and cities. By the year 2000, however, the urban population had grown to 2.9 billion, or 47 per cent of the population, and by 2025, there will be 4.9 billion people, no less than 60 per cent of the world's population, living in towns and cities. Poor people are drawn into cities because they provide opportunities for work and employment. That is why 2 billion people are set to flood into the already crowded cities of the developing world over the next twenty-five years. But taking up the opportunities for work that cities offer too often means having to bring up one's children in the squalid surroundings of a slum or a shanty town and to endure the consequent effects of social injustice and division. In Africa, 56 per cent of the urban population currently live in slums, in Asia the figure is 37 per cent, and in Latin America it is no less than 76 per cent. Compare that to the 4 per cent of the urban population who live in slums in Europe, and the 1 or 2 per cent in the United States, and you will see why slums are overwhelmingly a problem for the developing world. Moreover, the rapidity with which cities of the developing world are set to grow means that they present a greater challenge than rural areas in the fight against poverty.

What exactly are 'slums' in these cities? For a precise description, we need look no further than the work of the Cities Alliance. The main initiative of the Cities Alliance, an urban development coalition created by the World Bank and UN-HABITAT in 1999, has been its Cities Without Slums action plan, which has transformed work in this area, and to which I shall come back later. The Cities Alliance defines 'slums' in the following terms:

Slums are neglected parts of cities where housing and living conditions are appallingly poor. They range from high density, squalid central city tenements to spontaneous squatter settlements without legal recognition or rights, sprawling at the edge of cities. Some are more than fifty years old, some are land invasions just underway [. . .] Slums do not have: basic municipal services such as water, sanitation, waste collection, storm drainage, street lighting, paved footpaths, and roads for emergency access; schools and clinics within easy reach; safe areas for children to play; or places for the community to meet and socialize [. . .] Visible disparities between slums and better-off neighbourhoods increase the social tensions in poorer areas.[4]

Slums are the theatres of social division in the cities of the developing world, the physical manifestation of bad policies and social exclusion. The case of Maria Vargas, which I quoted earlier, shows how exposed slums are to the worst effects of crime, disease, and natural disasters. In many cities of the developing world, they are not merely small pockets of poverty, but vast zones that cover areas larger than the planned parts of the city itself. The prevailing impression that the visitor has on driving into such cities as São Paulo, Rio, and Nairobi is, quite simply, that the slums predominate.

Slums have different names in different parts of the world—'shanties', *kampungs, tugurios, bidonvilles, favelas*—but they all force their inhabitants to live in the same injustice and squalor.

What is to be done about these slums? Here too, as in the field of development more generally, the thinking has changed in recent years. Many mayors and urban practitioners used to believe that the best thing to do with a slum was simply to get rid of it in order to redevelop the area. But what, in that case, would become of the residents of that slum? The solution was essentially the same: 'let's clear them out too and send them somewhere else, these people without rights, these people who are disrupting our city planning. They don't exist legally, so let's be rid of them.' (More common was: 'send them back to where they came from'.) Removing people has never been a solution and invariably tends to make the problem worse. In almost all cases, the problem of the divided city—in which areas of affluence and entitlement coexist with the most appalling slums—did not just refuse to go away; it actually got worse. Only then did some mayors finally start to face the problem squarely. They did so, once again, not out of altruism so much as out of self-interest. It was much harder for them to attract investment to the city they had been elected to govern when potential investors looked out of the window of their fancy hotel and saw slums stretching away for miles on end. Nothing is more likely to make an investor go elsewhere. Who, after all, is going to want to invest in a city where bodyguards shadow the wealthier locals wherever they go and where they live in houses protected by high wire fences, alarms, and CCTV cameras? These are the walls that divide cities in Latin America and other parts of the developing world today. City mayors have now understood that these walls block incoming investment as well as greater social cohesion. The sea change in the approach to slums is essentially the same one that has transformed thinking about the problem of poverty in the developing world as a whole. Just as the world now understands that grinding poverty in one part affects all the others, so the inhabitants of a given city have come to recognize that they are all subject to the ill effects of poverty wherever it exists in their city. Mayors now realize that they were elected to run a city, not just its rich neighbourhoods, and that the city of today and tomorrow is and must be nothing less than the entire city.

This sea change in thinking is reflected in the recent commitment made by all those affected to address together the problem of slums. The Cities Without Slums action plan of the Cities Alliance is the direct result of this global commitment. The action plan is not directed towards the removal of slums and their inhabitants but, rather, towards what is called 'citywide slum upgrading'. This means giving all slum dwellers the chance to remain in the part of the city that they have established as their own while also helping them to develop the services and amenities and the sense of ownership that transform a slum into a healthy urban community. Slum upgrading typically involves:

- installing or improving basic infrastructure such as water, waste collection, and electricity;
- mitigating the threat of environmental disaster;
- improving access to health care and education;
- supporting programmes that protect citizens against crime and violence;
- constructing community facilities such as nurseries, health posts, and open spaces;

- regularizing security of tenure;
- enhancing income-earning opportunities through training and micro-credit; and
- building the institutional framework to sustain improvements.[5]

Most crucially, slum upgrading means giving slum dwellers the security and stability necessary to invite them to invest in their own communities: it is the local investment of the slum dwellers and the private sector, even more than international aid, that policy-makers need to target. Slum upgrading has been endorsed at the highest political levels as a key target in the fight against poverty. The Cities Without Slums action plan was adopted by world leaders in 2000 as target 11 of the Millennium Development Goals: 'by 2020, to have achieved a significant improvement in the lives of at least 100 million slum dwellers as proposed in the "Cities Without Slums" initiative'.[6] Progress in the implementation of this urban target will be monitored through two indicators: the proportion of people who have access to basic sanitation, and of those who enjoy secure tenure. The Cities Without Slums initiative does not just provide a target for the reduction of urban poverty and a means of measuring progress made, but also, and crucially, an approach to the problem which reflects the new development paradigm described earlier. This approach is based around the forging of partnerships in the cities between all the main actors in the fight against urban poverty: international agencies, national and city governments, civil society, the private sector, and slum residents themselves, based on a recognition of the right of slum dwellers to be in the city, and to contribute socially and economically to its development. The task ahead is enormous, and no one underestimates the

difficulties. But the Cities Without Slums initiative nevertheless represents a significant advance in thinking about the
divided cities of the developing world and it offers their
poorest citizens a real chance.

I want, in the rest of this chapter, to show how this initiative
is making a difference, by singling out five crucial elements in
the process of slum upgrading. The first concerns the role of
government. I have already argued that a proper legal and
judicial framework, viable financial systems, freedom from
corruption, and the other conditions that make for good
government are essential requirements for any country that
wishes to make the most of its opportunities for development.
The same, it is worth stressing, applies equally to any city with
the same ambition. Brazil and South Africa are two developing countries that both have statutes in their Constitution
relating to cities. Such developments help create the conditions for good urban government. How do developments
such as these come about? They are, above all, caused by acts
of political will. The recent example of Brazil is, once again,
eloquent. After decades in which its many of its wealthiest
inhabitants used their huge political power effectively to
ignore the frailty of the country's position, suddenly, in what
must surely be regarded as a revolutionary turn in events,
52 million people voted to elect someone as president whom
the wealthy in Brazil long regarded as a dangerous radical. He
is now perceived by many as a political visionary. The election
of President Lula shows what can be achieved when the
people of a country expresses its democratic will for political
change, just as the April 1994 election of Nelson Mandela
signalled the democratic mandate for the transformation of
South Africa. Just as there was in South Africa nearly a decade
ago, there is now in Brazil a new belief in politics of a kind

that would have been inconceivable in the period prior to the last election. That has direct consequences for cities such as Rio de Janeiro and São Paulo, whose Bairro Legal Programme is one of the many worldwide currently being supported by the Cities Alliance.[7]

The second crucial element in successful slum upgrading is training. Mayors and other city officials capable of competently managing such a process need to be nurtured and trained. This issue will become particularly important as the world's biggest cities rapidly expand to become megalopolises. In 1950, there was one city with a population of over 10 million people, New York City, with 12.3 million. By 2015, there will be twenty-one such megalopolises, seventeen of them in developing countries. The numbers projected express the size of the problem: by 2015, Dacca (Bangladesh) will have a population of 32.8 million; Mumbai (India), 22.6 million; São Paolo (Brazil), 21.2 million; Delhi (India), 20 million; Mexico City (Mexico), 20 million; Chicago (USA), 17 million; and Calcutta (India), 26 million. Cities containing 20 million people will effectively be countries-within-countries. Governing them will mean facing the same issues that national governments face. The difference, however, will be that, in these megalopolises, the delivery of services and management will be in the hands not of national governments but of city mayors. Mayors and officials in local government will suddenly find themselves in the frontline of the global fight against poverty. Yet, until now, they have not been trained for such a task.

That is why the World Bank and its partners are putting so much effort and expertise into training people to govern towns and cities all over the world. Every Saturday morning in Monterrey (Mexico), to give one example, the World Bank runs courses for mayors of towns and villages in seven countries of the region. Textbooks in Spanish are sent out to all the participants. These cover everything from organizing an election, chairing a meeting, running a fire department, and managing sewage collection to the provision of health services. The Bank decided to provide, in addition to the courses themselves, a website with a 'notice board' on which participants could post their questions directly. The success of the website was something that no one could quite have expected. Mayors from across the seven countries started using the website notice board to share the fruits of their knowledge and experience and to solve their problems together without needing to have recourse to the Bank's experts. So a mayor of a town in Chile, say, explains on the website one morning that his or her police department is experiencing problems because its cars are constantly breaking down. The mayor, instead of suffering alone as before, now finds thirty replies on the website the following morning from fellow mayors who have either run into the same problem, or who have a cousin who does a good deal on replacement cars, or who know from personal experience that it is nothing more serious than a problem with the carburettors. Cooperation of this kind between mayors in seven developing countries happens every day out of Monterrey. During a recent trip I made to Brazil, the World Bank started a network designed to link up 3 thousand cities and towns throughout the country by internet and video conferencing. Such initiatives make dialogue between practitioners possible in a new way. Universities also have a role to play. In June 2002, the Cities Alliance joined forces with the Massachusetts Institute of Technology (MIT) to present a week-long training course on slum upgrading. Participants came from projects in

Brazil, Mexico, India, South Africa, Cambodia, Vietnam, the Philippines, and Madagascar. This course is part of a wider initiative to marshal the intellectual and institutional resources of universities and practitioners in different parts of the world in order to form the mayors and urban development experts of the future.

These first two crucial elements in slum upgrading, mentioned so far, are both at the level of government. The remaining elements concern living conditions for slum dwellers themselves. The third is the provision of basic services. This makes an immediate and enormous difference to the quality of life for the urban poor. It removes at one stroke, for example, the sources of the contagious diseases that strike disproportionate numbers of slum dwellers in Africa, Asia, and Latin America.

The fourth element is the provision of secure tenure for the urban poor.[8] This is perhaps the most important thing that the other partners in urban development can offer slum dwellers. The urban poor have become accustomed to being treated as if they had no right of tenure, in fact, as if they had no rights at all. They need to know that where they live now is going to remain home for them in the future. Secure tenure offers a sense of inclusion, stability, and security. It says to the urban poor: 'you have a right to remain in the place you call home'. Sometimes all that is needed is for tenure to be guaranteed for a brief period of time. I discussed the problem recently with a colleague of mine who governed the city of Ahmedabad in India. He told me that, in an attempt to provide basic services to the urban poor living in a slum community called Sanjaynagar, he and his colleagues had developed a programme called *Parivartan* or 'Change'. This programme, instead of attempting to eradicate the slums and to displace those who lived in them, offered the slum dwellers the chance of tenure. An announcement was made to the entire population of Sanjaynagar: 'the city is suspending all prosecutions relating to illegal occupation of land for the next ten years. You are free to stay here for all of that time, whoever you are, and wherever you live.' The announcement brought a flourishing response. The city raised money both from its poorest residents and from outside to start a programme of slum upgrading in Sanjaynagar. This made the provision of services such as sewerage and water possible. It also encouraged the residents to participate actively in the slum-upgrading programme. The beauty of doing upgrading in this way, as happens in India, Mexico, South Africa, Mauritania, Morocco, Brazil, and in many other countries, is that it gives the people in the community a sense of belonging to a community, of owning something, of having a voice.

While giving property titles empowers the poor, it also takes time. But similar benefits can be achieved by giving them other more immediate forms of secure tenure. Results from all over the world show that, if local authorities offer secure tenure to the urban poor and then start providing them with basic services, the poor will in turn start investing in their community. In fact, the statistics on a global basis show that every dollar invested by the authorities in slum upgrading yields no less than seven dollars of investment from the residents of the slum. This explodes the myth that people in poverty have no money. It also indicates the importance of including the urban poor in the development process.

This was brought home to me on my first trip to the slums or *favelas* that cling to the steep sides of the mountains around Rio de Janeiro. I was visiting a *favela* in which the Bank had recently completed the installation of a water and sewerage system. What did this mean for the people of the *favela*, I asked? It meant, as they explained to me, that they no longer had to climb down and back up the mountain to fetch water. It meant too that neither they nor their children were constantly prone to illness and disease. Both improvements bought crucial time and energy for these people to work and so increase their income. Secure tenure has the same effect. Why so? Because those who do not have tenure are forced to stay at home for fear that someone may occupy their home while they are out at work, and they do not trust anyone to protect their house in their absence. Many of those interviewed in the *Voices of the Poor* study said that they did not know whether to turn to the police or to the criminals for protection. Secure tenure and access to basic services do not simply offer the urban poor more time and energy. They offer, more fundamentally, the recognition that the poorest citizens are entitled to a place in society. This recognition takes many forms. Many of the women I met during my trip to the *favelas* in Rio were keen to present me with the receipt proving that they had paid their water bill. What they were in fact showing me was the first official document that bore their names. Having such a document meant that they could go down into Rio and buy a bicycle or apply for a bank loan because, for the first time in their lives, they could offer proof of address. It meant that they were, all of a sudden, recognized members of society. Secure tenure is the beginning of an end to social division and, with political will, can be implemented with very little cost or difficulty.

The fifth and final element in slum upgrading is the provision of financial services. These need to be made available both to the urban poor and, at the level of local government, to the city mayors. Two forms of lending to the urban poor are proving particularly successful: the first is micro-credit, which allows people to start small businesses; the second is a three-year loan of anything up to about 1,500 dollars for people who wish to invest in improvements to their own houses. The repayment rates on these loans are remarkably high because people in slums, more so even than in the richer counterparts of the city, feel sure that losing their house is the last thing they want happen to them. So they pay.[9] These are two new developments in the provision of financial services to the urban poor. At a higher financial level, a coalition of development partners, including the British and Swedish Governments and the World Bank, is currently devising a scheme that requires a portion of development assistance to be set aside for the construction of low-cost houses for the poorest residents. Such schemes help make a place for these residents within society. Mayors and city planners used to regard such people as nothing and wanted to get them out of the way because they contravened the rules and regulations set for affluent areas of the city. Now they understand that poor people need to be given only a sense of dignity, not charity, to become responsible and productive citizens.

To finish, let us return to the case of Maria Vargas, the single mother of many sons living near São Paolo in the *favela* of Sacadura Cabral, where poverty and social exclusion are facts of life, and where many of the residents lack secure tenure. One of Maria's sons, Fernando, was also interviewed as part of the *Voices of the Poor* study. Fernando holds out great hope that he will be able to improve life in Sacadura. He started work at the age of 8 in a textile factory, but now, aged 21, dreams of becoming a judge. He wishes to study the law, because, in his view, the people of the *favela* need education and an active role in society if they are to have a future. He says: 'in a *favela*, people have no idea of their rights. We have police discrimination, the politicians abuse us, and others use their knowledge to take advantage of us. So I want to know all about rights and obligations.'[10] Fernando's aspirations for the urban slum of Sacadura Cabral are those that must drive reform and development in cities all over the developing world. For they produce cities without slums.

Conclusion

Cities tended in the past to display the most pernicious effects of poverty in the developing world. They were divided between centres of enormous power and affluence and slums whose inhabitants were denied exercise of their rights for the simple reason that, in the eyes of the so-called 'legal' urban dwellers (who sometimes and in some places are in the majority and other times are not), they did not even exist. Today, thanks in general to a welcome shift in the development paradigm and in particular to the Cities Without Slums action plan, there is a new recognition throughout the developing world that the urban poor have not only rights but, what is more, an essential part to play in building the city of tomorrow. We must all join with them if we are to make the city truly undivided.

5

Introduction to Richard Rogers

James Attlee

It is surprising how few architects have come to grips with the crisis that faces the contemporary city. Richard Rogers is an exception. Over the last thirty years or so, the buildings that have made Rogers famous have been, as much as anything, explorations of the principles that have concerned him: flexibility, modernity, inclusivity, and sustainability. At the same time, in his writings and public discourse, he has been a passionate advocate of the city as a place of social and intellectual interchange, a democratic and architecturally stimulating environment. This vision is rooted as much in the civic ideals of the Italian Renaissance—Rogers was born in Florence—as in the late twentieth-century avant-garde. Many of the changes to the public face of London that have taken place over the last decade—the opening up of the river and the pedestrianization of Trafalgar Square are two examples—were called for by Rogers in architectural proposals, writings, and public statements published since the 1980s. Architecture, he has argued, cannot be detached from social and political issues. Increasingly, his words have had a prophetic edge, befitting his senior status within the profession and the cultural life of the nation. As one of the best-known architects on the planet, Rogers, at least potentially, has the ear of both government and business, the twin agencies holding the future of the urban landscape in their hands. For this reason alone, what he has to say merits close attention.

Rogers first came to international prominence with the opening of the Pompidou Centre in the Beauborg area of central Paris, designed with his then partner, Renzo Piano, in 1976. One of the key buildings of the twentieth century, it changed the face of the French capital, creating a new cultural heart of the city. Rogers's banishment of services to external ducts, creating vast open interior spaces, was to become a trademark further developed in the Lloyds Building in London, completed in 1984. Both structures celebrate urban life and activity, although one is a public and one a private space. The Beauborg has been compared to a giant climbing frame. Many of its visitors never enter the art gallery and library it contains, but merely ride the external elevators to enjoy the view, while the vast piazza around it resembles a cross between a Renaissance square, a market-place, and a playground. The Lloyds Building, its gleaming steel exterior punctuating the stone and glass façades of its surroundings as though the internal mechanisms of the city itself had been exposed, grants the pedestrian views of workers ascending heavenwards, like angels, in external lifts. Both buildings were designed to be energy efficient, flexible, and future-proofed for changing requirements. In microcosm this reflects Rogers's view of the city, which, he believes, should adapt to the needs of its inhabitants, rather than the other way around. These principles are to be developed further in his latest landmark City of London project, a 48-floor tapered glass tower immediately adjoining his most famous British structure, the Lloyds Building. In a gesture typical of Rogers's libertarian instincts, the site will include half an acre of public space, granting public access and a moment of civic freedom in a district characterized by police checkpoints, doormen, and security guards. The 736-foot-high transparent 'spire' will face off with London's newest internationally recognized architectural icon, the Swiss Rea 'Gherkin' at 30 St Mary Axe, designed by Rogers's old partner from Team 4, Norman Foster.

The commissions undertaken by the Richard Rogers Partnership around the world over the last two decades have not been free of controversy. One need think of only three recent or current projects in Britain, the Millennium Dome, Terminal 5 at Heathrow, and the Welsh Assembly building, to realize that the major-league architects of the twenty-first century have to be prepared to fight their corner with all comers. This argumentative dynamism is now brought to bear on those who decide the shape of future urban development in Britain. Rogers has been Chair of the Urban Task Force at a time when Britain faces its greatest architectural challenge since the era of post-war reconstruction. Within the next twenty years, sites for four million new households must be found in our already overcrowded island. Before the developers are let off the leash, some serious thinking has to be done. What kind of society are we hoping to build?

It is a truism that Modernism's main failure was its concentration on creating the perfect building, while ignoring the way that building slotted into a complex grid of streets, neighbourhoods, and communities. The vital 'negative space' between structures, the space inhabited by pedestrians on the way to local shops or by children walking to school, has been largely abandoned to planners at local council level, creating an environment rendered increasingly hostile by heavy car use and crime. Rogers has undertaken extensive research on the health of urban Britain, and his findings should make uncomfortable reading for those that govern us. Swathes of our major cities have been abandoned by a population that has emigrated to the suburbs. Those left behind often inhabit communities deprived of proper services or local amenities, surrounded by semi-derelict buildings, and prey to vandalism. He highlights the need for a more holistic, '3-D' approach to city planning, made possible through a better level of training for planners and architects and greater public participation in local democracy. To pump funding into an ailing school, he suggests, while failing to address the decay in the neighbourhood that surrounds it, is like trying to stand a stool on two legs. He correctly identifies the lifting of controls on out-of-town developments during the 1980s as having had a devastating effect on local economies, sucking the life out of town centres already decimated by the collapse of manufacturing. Wal-Mart, currently poised for expansion in the United Kingdom, have more people in uniform than the United States Armed Forces.

So what of the alternatives that Rogers proposes? He calls for densely populated city centres with excellent transport links and key amenities within walking distance of each other, and for the redevelopment of urban, brownfield sites, rather than an increasing expansion into an already overburdened countryside. As sincerely as a fifteenth-century Florentine senator, he believes that beautiful architecture in a city promotes civic responsibility in its citizens. In the age of the information superhighway, he argues, there should be no need for workers to make highly polluting journeys outside their own communities. This vision, blending ecological concerns and awareness of the latest technology with an urban model rooted in pre-industrial Europe, has much to recommend it. Car use, which increasingly includes short journeys to local facilities or the transport of children to school, is one of the principal causes of global warming, the stalking nightmare of our age. However, the benefits delivered by information technology have not been quite as originally envisioned. Increasingly miniaturized and complex devices allow workers to be more, not less, mobile. The office is portable, not based in the home. We live in a hyper-mobile society and have exported our paradigm to the developing world: the average journey time to work in Jakarta is three hours; car ownership in Beijing is growing at 25 per cent each year. A kind of evolution has taken place whereby workers, like certain kinds of birds and animals, are prepared to migrate vast distances from their homes each day to provide for their needs. Not for nothing was the first Rotterdam Architecture Biennial in 2003 entitled 'Mobility: A Room with a View'. The 'room' that the Biennial's title referred to has four wheels; motorways are the most frequently visited public spaces in many European countries. Architect Will Alsop has argued that to resist the supremacy of road transport is futile, as the train network will never return to a level of dependability that serves the public's needs. Instead we should create 'super-cities' along the axes of the motorway network that join together urban conurbations, trading local identity for membership of a megalopolis, embracing the very outward expansion of the city that Rogers decries.

Can Rogers's vision resist pressure from these new models, each of which argues that it is the most attuned to the reality of today's society? Can the workforce be weaned away from their habit of automotive mobility? More pertinently, can jobs that deliver sufficient income to satisfy our consumerist desires be created in every community? And can affordable housing be provided in the areas where work is concentrated? These are big issues that can be resolved only through a high level of government intervention in the so-called 'free' market. So far only a handful of the recommendations in the report produced by the Urban Task Force have been taken up as policy. Rogers has nonetheless been given a unique opportunity to influence the formation of government thinking. The real question is not over the good sense of the measures he proposes. Rather it is whether, in this age of the devolution of governmental responsibility to the private sector, the political will exists to make them a reality. The late Edward Said famously stated that the role of the intellectual was to 'speak truth to power'. What role remains for the prophetic voice when a power vacuum lies at the heart of government?

An Urban Renaissance

Richard Rogers

Urban living lies at the heart of our society. Cities are meeting places for people, whether friends or strangers, and for the exchange of ideas. The beginnings of civic society can be traced back some 5 thousand years to the banks of the Tigris and the Euphrates, where the concepts of citizenship and civil rights were born. Cities today embody the dominant moral force guiding our civilization: they are the framework of society, the generators of civic values and the civil society, the cultural and economic command centres of our world. Active citizens gather in them to build political structures and a corresponding human environment. In cities, the social and the physical are intimately linked, for better or worse: Hellenic Athens, Renaissance Florence, eighteenth-century Paris, Georgian London, and contemporary Barcelona all combined the beauty of urban space with the concept of civic society; at the same time, there are many cities of the past and present in which the ghettos of the rich and the slums of the poor have engendered nothing but division and strife.

Of the global population, 50 per cent now live in cities. A hundred years ago this figure was a mere 10 per cent, whereas in fifty years' time it will have soared to 75 per cent. After Bangladesh and Holland, England is the most densely populated country in the world, and has a major stake in containing city growth and the conservation of what precious countryside remains. This is because urban sprawl and out-of-town development suck the vitality from our cities, reducing what should be humankind's most complex and dynamic artefact into dehumanized and crime-infested ghettos. This chapter proposes a vision of the sustainable compact city for the twenty-first century. There is in many respects nothing new about this vision. A typical example of a medieval city reveals that, in essence, the basic language of urban landscape has not dramatically altered: it is organized around the central square, the church, the town hall, the market space, the network of roads, and above all the need for public space. The medieval city was a highly compact urban organism in which people could live, work, play, and interact with one another. If the Renaissance represented a peak in the evolution of the city (think of Florence or London), the Industrial Revolution turned cities into the unliveable hell so vividly conjured up by Dickens and Daumier: dark places where, in 1841, the average life expectancy was less than twenty years. Politicians and the great architects, planners, and urban theorists from Ebeneezer Howard to Le Corbusier, plus a whole generation of post-World War II governments, were all fundamentally opposed to the city. As a result, those who could afford to flee the pollution and degradation of city life moved to outlying suburbs, new towns, and the countryside, initiating a mass exodus that has radically eroded our cities and our sense of citizenship.

How can we improve the quality of our towns and cities today? If ever a country were crying out for a culture of sustainable cities, it is the UK. A terrifying suburban sprawl threatens to destroy a significant proportion of the UK's precious countryside while simultaneously stripping inner cities of all vitality or direction. When people, shops, and jobs desert inner-city areas, the poor are left to inhabit ghost towns that are desolate, socially deprived, and fragmented. Many of our major cities are host to derelict and lifeless inner-city estates, shabby suburban sprawl, and dirty and squalid streets. My practice recently made a study of the eastern area of Manchester, one of the great industrial cities of the nineteenth century. The decline of manufacturing throughout the latter part of the twentieth century dealt cities such as Manchester a double body blow: it suffered not only the physical legacy of the industrial era but also the social problems of mass unemployment. As a result, the population of East Manchester has dropped from about 80,000 immediately after World War II to only 18,000 today. Of every five houses, four are boarded up, and most urban entrepreneurs are leaving. Anyone who can get out does so, hopping over the green belt areas and moving into the suburbs. The result is an inner city area rapidly transformed into a ghost town, deprived of facilities. Compounding the problem, our cities have the highest traffic congestion, the longest commuting times, the worst public transport, and the most expensive housing in Europe. It is no surprise that the middle-income majority leave city centres to find clean air, better schools, and a decent environment in which to bring up their children. Who can blame them? Our cities, which for years attracted the best and brightest people and were the epitome of our hopes and ambitions, are being badly eroded. An acute housing shortage, a fractured and failing transport system, huge tracts of as yet underdeveloped brownfield sites, badly designed housing estates rife with poverty and crime: this scenario, sadly, is typical of many dysfunctional cities in the UK, characterized by traffic and pollution, poor schooling, graffiti, and litter. People are voting with their feet.

The good news is that in 1997, after enduring decades of complacency and public squalor, the British people elected a government that cares about cities and citizens. For the first time, central and local government have taken on the challenge of an urban renaissance, stressing the need for sustainable communities rather than shouting for more houses. There is a huge amount of work to do.

Three Drivers for Urban Change

Our post-industrial urban society is being driven by three principles of change.

• The global information network is strengthening the corporate market worldwide, often at the cost of the less fortunate, eroding the power of nations, and encouraging the emergence of a constellation of global cities. This also allows us to examine a large number of case studies, from Bombay to Phoenix and from Curitiba to Barcelona.

• The alteration of family life is making us more urban. Developed countries are characterized by divorce rates at nearly 50 per cent, an average of just over two children per family, and life expectancy of nearly eighty years, roughly double what it was a century ago. The effect of these statistics will be to change the fundamental structure of our global community. Lengthy retirement, the need for life-long learning, a radical shift in the ratio between work and leisure, the weakening of the family unit, and the strengthening of the individual: these factors will all attract people back into our cities.

• We are taking our environmental responsibilities more seriously. The earth is a live organism, not an inorganic material, and we must learn to look after and nurture our environment rather than despoil it. Whatever action we take today has to be seen in the context of future effects. Waste, for instance, is a critical factor in terms of the global economy. Energy can be divided into two kinds: energy stored in carbon fuel over time, which is massively polluting and dangerous to our future existence on this planet; clean fuel, primarily the sun, the wind, and the earth itself. Scientific research could deliver us clean energy, but there is massive corporate interest in keeping things as they are.

Twenty-first-century cities need to respond more closely to our current needs by being transformed into well-designed, higher-density urban environments in which public services can work effectively and a broad mix of people can live together. The benefits of cohesive communities are self-evident: safety and civic pride promote what De Tocqueville famously called 'the habit of association'. Mixed-use developments, shops lining streets, homes overlooking attractively landscaped public spaces, parks, and playgrounds, and people walking and cycling all make for cities that are ecologically sustainable, economically strong, and socially inclusive.

The Urban Task Force

England alone needs more than 4 million more households over the next twenty years. Of that figure, 80 per cent are required for single-person households, an indication of huge social changes. It is vital to understand that the vast majority of these changes can be accommodated by denser urban planning on brownfield land and by better use of existing buildings. The UK faces an economic situation in which housing and employment are creating a boom in the South-East and bust in the North. Better fast trains from South to North and North-West would improve the situation. So would the creation of new jobs and better entertainment amenities in beautiful cities such as Bath and Brighton. But a radical change in attitude is urgently needed as well: people should be encouraged to remain in existing cities, such as Birmingham, which already have schools, hospitals, police, public transport, and of course quantities of brownfield land, rather than creating new towns. The government policy of developing new urban zones in places such as Milton Keynes, Peterborough, and Basildon should be re-examined. If we continue to allow new developments to encroach on greenfield land, the cost to the Treasury in hidden subsidy will be prodigious (an average of £40,000 per home), to say nothing of the damage to our environment and community, the cost of additional roads and utilities, the waste of time spent in traffic, the effect of greater travel time on accident victims and those with disabilities, and the loss of productive rural land.

In order to address the state of our cities and especially the housing crisis in the UK, the Prime Minister, Tony Blair, and the Deputy Prime Minister, John Prescott, asked me to chair a government task force that would identify the causes of urban decline, recommend practical ways of bringing people back into city centres, and provide 4 million additional homes without contributing to the growing erosion of greenfield sites. The Urban Task Force was formed in 1998. It was made up of sociologists, architects, developers, ecologists, land-use specialists, urban administrators, and city planners. It worked for about a year to produce the first major report on the subject for over two decades. The report's 105 recommendations are based on the principles of sustainable urban planning, design excellence, social well-being, and environmental responsibility within a viable economic and legislative framework. Its aim was to persuade the UK government to promote ways of facilitating greater urban density and better design in order to make city life desirable and sustainable. There are examples of such cities to be found all over the world, from Curitiba in Brazil to Portland, Oregon, and many British inner cities—London, Birmingham, Manchester, Leeds, and Glasgow—have started to undergo an urban Renaissance.

The eight key aspirations of the Urban Task Force, which were first published in *Cities for a Small Planet*,[1] were:

1. A compact city—with neighbourhoods encouraging vitality in public areas, a spirit of community, and providing home/work/play locations all within walking distance. New developments should be focused on brownfield sites within the city, whose outer limits should be clearly defined to restrict out-of-town expansion and protect the countryside.

2. A diverse city—in which social and physical integration are encouraged, and in which rich and poor live in the same neighbourhoods, through programmes of integrated and affordable housing.

3. A city of easy contact—thanks to a dynamic public realm, information exchange, and a fully integrated transport policy based on walking, cycling, and public transport.

4. A beautiful city—in which art, architecture, and land-scape spark the imagination and offer a strong sense of belonging and well-being; in which imagination and innovation are treasured, public space is revitalized, and the scale and grain of buildings create a play of light and shadow as the spirit of the city evolves.

5. An equitable city—in which social well-being is a given right, people can participate in local government, and justice, food, shelter, education, health, wealth, and hope are fairly distributed.

6. An ecologically sustainable city—encouraging climate control, biodiversity, and the efficient use of resources.

7. A well-ordered, adaptable city—in which civic pride is valued, government programmes contribute to urban regeneration, development is based on design-led strategic 3-D spatial planning, and sequential testing prioritizes brownfield development; in which planning institutions initiate creative integrated strategies on the strength of public, professional, and governmental participation; and in which research and innovation are encouraged with clear links between local, regional, and central government.

8. A city of economic strength—which generates and sustains jobs and investment, and whose leaders champion regeneration and realize new urban economic strategies.

The Urban Task Force Report 'Towards an Urban Renaissance', published in June 1999, in turn prompted the government's Urban White Paper, published in November 2000, incorporating many of our recommendations. The White Paper was of course only a first step, since implementation is the key to success, and this is largely dependent on legal action, long-term fiscal commitment, and education.

The Urban Task Force highlighted the need to limit further development of greenfield land by redeveloping urban brownfield sites and derelict buildings, the importance of improved urban design, better public transport, and an increased density which would support local services and create a stronger sense of local community and public safety. The challenge is to reverse the drift of people from city to country. Our aim should be to ensure that towns such as Birmingham, Manchester, Liverpool, and Newcastle start to gain population, not lose it.

The Challenge Ahead

Urban renaissance affects every citizen—from pensioners to children and from business leaders to people struggling with poverty—and every part of our civic life. The Government has invested in public programmes—in health, education, social inclusion, jobs, and the regional economy—but, if these initiatives are to flourish, the physical fabric of our towns and cities must be right. In truth, despite some successes, the government has not yet shown that it truly understands the role of the city in supporting the physical infrastructure of society. A vibrant built environment provides the glue that binds all other aspects of our collective existence together. A city or town that is degraded by neglect and underinvestment will breed ever-larger concentrations of poverty, resulting in massive social exclusion. This is why 'joined-up government' is so vital. We need a national urban policy, framed by the whole government, to provide the physical framework for other policies. We have welfare policies aimed at disadvantaged people as individuals—new deals for the unemployed, single mothers, and the disabled—but little to help the communities in which those people live.

Where is the money going? Over the past five years, local government spending on education has risen by more than 30 per cent and on police by 25 per cent. Government spending on the health service as a whole has risen by 60 per cent. But in contrast, local government spending on environmental services has risen by a meagre 17 per cent, merely keeping pace with inflation. The annual budget for schools and hospitals has risen by 50 billion pounds since 1997, yet local authorities have been allotted a mere 1 billion pounds more to spend on public spaces, streets, and parks, the fabric that holds our towns and cities together.

Without physical regeneration, we are trying to stand a stool on two legs and should not be surprised when it wobbles. The problems that beset many of our communities are not solely the result of the degraded physical state of our towns and cities, but they cannot be solved without reference to it. The built environment of our towns and cities provides the physical framework for all our institutions and government programmes. These will all fail unless we can deliver the physical context which allows them to flourish. The greatest difficulty I had with the UK government was in trying to persuade them that social exclusion goes hand in hand with physical dereliction and that one cannot be dealt with in isolation from the other. The government's own Social Exclusion Unit has now discovered that poverty can be addressed only in tandem with area dereliction. It is useless to invest in a single institution—such as a school—if most members of the local community are so dispirited by their surroundings that they are desperately trying to leave. The experience of the past two decades has proved that pouring money in an ad hoc fashion into squalid and fragmented inner city areas does not represent good value. The planning debate about the need for new homes and where to put them is often couched in terms of saving the countryside. But equally important should be our concern to save our cities. The mass exodus to the suburbs today continues to be driven by the poor quality of inner-city life. The complex demands of modern-day life have brought their own specific pressures to bear on the the existing urban fabric, and in many instances it cannot take the strain.

We have fallen way behind our European counterparts in terms of revitalizing our inner city areas and making urban life attractive. Europe's urban strategies over the last twenty years have demonstrated that the creation of public spaces and sustainable densities makes cities thrive. Amsterdam's new dockside residential development, Borneo Sporenberg, is clear proof, if any were needed, that investment in a well-designed built environment pays dividends. It is a classic example of a low-rise, high-density, beautiful neighbourhood. It is high time that we in the UK stopped flinching at the notion of 'beauty'. Architectural beauty transforms size into scale and matter into light, rhythm, and colour. Many European cities are triumphs of imaginative town planning. Quality of urban life is far better in Barcelona, Copenhagen, Düsseldorf, Amsterdam, Strasbourg, and Turin than in Birmingham, Manchester, or Newcastle, the best examples that England has to offer. Holland has the closest geography to that of England as well as very similar social problems, and is far more successful in achieving compact low-rise housing. I have been immensely impressed by what I have seen in The Hague. On my last visit, I walked around with local politicians, and the calibre of public and private housing was such that it was impossible to distinguish between them. This is a great achievement: in England, most social housing is arranged in ghettos, clearly identifiable from a long way off. Barcelona is another excellent example of creative urban planning: a compact, dense, and well-designed city, it is the jewel in the regeneration crown. It should be noted that such a transformation cannot happen overnight; Barcelona took fifteen years to turn around. But the city now attracts 9 million tourists each year, only 2 million less than Venice. More important is the reduction in court cases in Barcelona, a statistic which supports the theory that a well-designed urban environment breeds social cohesion. Barcelona is a city that, quite simply, works. Why? Because it has had the benefit of three visionary mayors who all recognized the importance of the spatial city and the social city and saw a way of marrying these two concepts.

The city is very much like a body. You can identify its component parts—communities, neighbourhoods, districts, and so on—and you can also diagnose its ills. A neighbourhood should have at least 5,000 people; that is about the minimum needed economically to support a bus, small shopping area, nursery, health clinic, and community hall. These focal areas should be within walking distance for all the inhabitants of the neighbourhood. A number of neighbourhoods makes a district, a number of districts adds up to a city centre, with each increase in scale supporting larger amenities. The city centre contains the Town Hall, university, cathedral, shopping centre, and so on.

Density is not necessarily synonymous with cramming. The difference between cramming and urban vitality is design. Large parts of Georgian London were built to densities of about 100 dwellings per hectare. But no one would claim that Georgian housing—with its tree-lined avenues, garden squares, and beautifully proportioned façades—is in any sense crammed. A good example of successful urban density is the early Victorian development in Notting Hill, London, one of the city's most dynamic and ethnically mixed neighbourhoods. Predominantly terraced housing is arranged around public gardens so that all households have access to green space and are within walking distance of shops and public transport. The area is extremely popular and nowadays house prices are high. This is testament to the long-term benefits of good design. In stark contrast, most modern developments in English suburbs rarely average more than twenty-three dwellings per hectare and in towns the figure is about thirty-five dwellings per hectare, the lowest density in Western Europe. Even a modest increase in density would dramatically alter the equation between the number of housing units and the amount of land they occupy. It would come from the correct balance of mass, light, and space. Good design produces density through long life, loose fit, and low energy buildings, not through quickly thrown up hermetically sealed boxes. The desirable quarters of the average city have very high densities: London's Mayfair, Park Avenue in New York, and the Avenue Foch in Paris (200 dwellings per hectare) are typical examples. Arguing about density levels on brownfield sites is academic: one must consider planning density in 3-D and relate it to the specific morphology and landscape of a given site. For example, a density increase of 20 per cent is only equivalent to adding one room in five, or doing an attic conversion. It is true that adding some 450,000 dwellings demands a much more complex network approach including the production of microflats, roof gardens, and terraces in flexible 3-D frameworks that make use of mass production and planning legislation. John Prescott's 'sustainable communities' policy is a big step forward. But his development of new towns at the cost of existing ones is a step in the wrong direction.

Changing attitudes to density will not be easy. The government must take the lead in reconsidering planning applications and modifying permissions to ensure higher densities and to encourage brownfield use before green. Contrary to a commonly held view, there is in fact enough brownfield land for most new development. Nationally, by using small infill sites of less than an acre, converting existing buildings, using roof spaces, and exploiting air rights, we can produce 35 to

50 per cent more homes before we even think of touching greenfield land. London is the fastest growing capital in the developed world, with a predicted 23 per cent increase between 1986 and 2016. Ken Livingstone, the Mayor of London, has stated that the extra three-quarters of a million people can all be housed inside London's existing thirty-three boroughs and within the limits of the very successful green belt that encloses the city. This is exactly what the Urban Task Force recommended.

But even areas in South-East England are not yet delivering their huge potential for integrated, intensive, and innovative mixed use development. The Thames Gateway—the largest 'reservoir' of brownfield land in the South East—is at this very moment being frittered away for lack of a holistic vision and a proper infrastructure (especially public transport). There is the opportunity to create a town for 300,000 people. But unless we treat this area holistically we will be lucky if we can achieve a third of that figure.

The biggest problem that we face is the lack of skills to deliver urban regeneration. In England, the art of urban planning has reached crisis point. If we fail to improve this situation, the Urban Renaissance will come to look like all the other post-war urban strategies, marginalized and forgotten. At present, decades of underinvestment have resulted in a serious lack of skills, particularly at the local level. We are a global society and should be drawing on the best talent from all over the world. The quality of the producers is crucial to the quality of the product. The UK's local authorities are fundamentally weak, lacking the necessary skills to design successful new housing and sustainable communities. Once you have decent architecture and urban design, you need good management, maintenance, and care of infrastructure. In

Palma, Majorca, the streets are cleaned three times a day; in Copenhagen, a third of the population uses bikes; in Strasbourg, civic pride is enhanced by a splendid tram system; in Barcelona, the corners of most city blocks include children's playgrounds and seats. But in Britain, our neighbourhoods are run down, the streets are strewn with litter and defaced with graffiti, and we appear to have no clear appreciation of the vital role that the Public Realm should play in our society. There is a tradition here of teaching planners to work only in two dimensions, instead of encouraging the use of 3-D spatial masterplans, and a reluctance to include social issues within the architectural syllabus. As a result, architects concentrate on vision and images, while planners have tremendous arguments about the mathematics of density without understanding the 3-D implications.

There is a real need for a national design framework. Masterplanners and architects can respond only to a given brief. Most of the design briefs I have seen for urban regeneration competition projects in the UK are disgraceful: they amount to no more than a couple of printed pages containing none of the facts necessary for a successful outcome. If the brief is poor, there is little hope for the solution; without an accurate diagnosis, there is little hope for the patient. The situation in the rest of Europe is quite different: a considerable amount of time and money is spent preparing the analysis and setting up the structure to run a successful team. The solution is simple: if we in the UK do not have the requisite knowledge, it is imperative that we import new blood, thereby re-educating ourselves to the level of our European counterparts. The setting up of the Commission for Architecture and the Built Environment may turn out to be the single most important step in improving the quality of design of our cities. It has already had an initial impact. But its powers are largely limited to recommendations for the improvement of buildings—especially public buildings—and the spaces between them.

Reduction of car use is a key factor in the urban renaissance. Cars are the antithesis of vibrant city life. It is no wonder that those living in 'hostile' environments take refuge in their cars. They are basically fortresses on wheels, and are a highly effective way of stopping people from engaging in all forms of communication, apart that is from the traded insults of road rage! Predictably, the American model of the city is the most petrol-greedy. Houston, Phoenix, and Detroit all create alarming levels of pollution. Urban sprawl with its dependence on car travel also has a direct effect on general health levels. The more people rely on cars, the less they walk, and the less fit they become. Recent studies in the US show that those living in sprawling urban areas are more likely to suffer from obesity, with increased risk of cancer, diabetes, higher blood pressure, and heart disease. The typical European city is, in contrast, far more energy-efficient. The process of reducing car use in cities depends on a series of interlinked factors such as compactness of development, public transport, speed control, secure and attractive routes for pedestrians, cyclists, and vehicles, and the cost of driving and parking. So ingrained is the car as an acceptable part of the general social structure that car-related death tolls are seemingly viewed as a 'natural' part of modern life. There are 2,600 road deaths in England every year, to say nothing of annual car-related injuries, which amount to over 300,000. Although these figures far outweigh annual deaths caused by more sensational plane and train accidents, they seem to go unnoticed. If we valued human life more, there are many ways in which we could reduce the number of accidents. Lower speed limits would have a dramatic effect, of course, and there is a real need for zones around schools and housing where cars may not travel faster than 20 mph. The UK government must also ensure that planners and developers take full account of the types of travel that any new development will generate. Local transport plans should be placed on a statutory footing, required to set specific targets for reducing the length and number of car journeys.

Ease of transport is a basic ingredient of successful urban planning. In Holland, public transport services are excellent and cycling is encouraged. In Copenhagen, where it is dark and cold for many months of the year, a third of the population goes by bicycle, a third by public transport, and (only) a third by car: the well-designed, secure streets are full of pedestrians. In England, most people avoid cycling because of its inherent dangers—the figures speak for themselves. Only 2 per cent of our population dares to use a bike, which means we have the lowest number of cyclists in Europe. In 1971, nearly all 7- and 8-year-olds walked or were walked to school. By 1993, practically nobody was walking to school: most were going by car and a few were using public transport. This is a direct reflection of the steady disintegration of the social fabric and it is also hugely wasteful of energy and a source of significant inner-city congestion and pollution. As a child, the best part of my day was that spent walking to and from school, kicking a ball around with my friends. This level of social interaction is lost once the need for a car becomes paramount, and all sense of community is sacrificed in the process.

Good governance is another vital element in the cities of tomorrow. The UK, which suffers from what is arguably the most centralized government in Western Europe, needs a national framework that enables and promotes urban regeneration but also the local political structures that can deliver it. The Labour government is carrying out a series of devolutionary steps which, though not yet forceful enough, will strengthen city and regional government. That alone will not make sustainable cities possible. The practical realization of a true urban renaissance depends on the requisite legislation and funding combined with visionary civic leadership. Civic leaders can fulfil their vision only if they are supported by the right powers and resources. They also need the support and participation of those who have elected them. The idea of widespread participation by citizens in the life of their city is crucial. The Architecture Foundation, an architectural centre in London, ran a series of debates two or three years ago. We thought we might attract 200 people to each event. But in the end 3,000 people turned up and, with that size of audience, we were able to attract speakers of the highest calibre such as Tony Blair and the mayors of New York and Barcelona. Today, fewer and fewer people are voting. We need to keep thinking about how to create a more engaged democratic society. The UK has a great deal of catching up to do if it is to create neighbourhoods whose inhabitants participate actively in the shaping of their own communities. The keyword is 'participation' and achieving this requires the empowering of local groups. The Netherlands are developing sophisticated techniques of public participation at all levels, from the local community and the neighbourhood right through to the city and the state. They have thirty-nine architectural centres for a population of 14 million. In this country, we are trying to serve some 50 million people with only eight architectural centres, each one of which is desperately short of money. But we need such institutions to support a more widspread public debate about the present and future of our cities.

Conclusion: A Vision for the Future

There is much still to do, but I am far more optimistic in this new climate of change. There have been some notable successes: the increasing use of brownfield areas for urban development and the discouragement of out-of-town shopping centres; cultural urban regeneration initiatives such as Salford's Imperial War Museum and Lowry Centre, the Baltic in Newcastle, Tate Modern in London; the establishment of the Commission for Architecture and the Built Environment to champion design quality in public buildings and new housing; changes to the tax system promoting urban excellence and regeneration opportunities; and finally all the social programmes aimed at improving the quality of life of the poor and the socially excluded.

We have a great opportunity to accommodate our growing population and revive our cities. But we are not there yet. I will end by listing seven urban priorities:

1. Use fiscal and legal strategies to make brownfield sites more attractive than green to developers. This should allow us to increase the percentage of brownfield development from 60 to 75 per cent in the first instance. We could set a target of 100 per cent in many places if incentives and regulations were in place and properly enforced. London under Ken Livingstone's leadership has already done just that.

2. Match increases in education and health with commensurate investment in the physical infrastructure that supports urban communities. An increase of £1 billion over

the past five years is not good enough. It barely keeps pace with inflation.

3. Give local authorities the powers, resources, and skills to deliver urban renaissance while ensuring that they are directly accountable to their citizens.

4. Focus on and invest in the quality of design of our public realm, as well as our housing, to create comfortable and beautiful spaces and buildings.

5. Increase regional participation. Central government, through the Office of the Deputy Prime Minister, should redirect the Regional Development Authorities to take a major role in directing physical, social, and economic regeneration. It should give them a new brief and help them to acquire the right skills, or set up new agencies that can rise to the challenge.

6. Develop a network of Regional Resource Centres for Urban Development, promoting innovation and good practice, coordinating urban development training and encouraging community participation in the regeneration process. Enable every city to have an architecture centre.

7. Establish joint working between professional institutions and education providers to develop a plan of action for improving skills.

A lot has changed since we published 'Towards an Urban Renaissance' in 1999: we have new institutions such as Regional Development Agencies, new mechanisms such as public service agreements, and cross-departmental initiatives such as Neighbourhood Renewal. These show that tightly focused interventions can make a difference. But all this good work will ultimately be wasted if it is not part of a wider integrated vision.

I do not believe that cities have outlived their role, nor that their growing abandonment is inevitable. Although the explosion in information technology, in theory, creates the opportunity for dispersal, remote communication, and virtual networks, many of those whose jobs rely on technology also require high mobility, core city services, and swift interchange. Cities provide the hub for the new communications network on which modern businesses increasingly depend. Many people would prefer to live near their place of work, as the strong revival of city centres all over the country shows. City centres are full of cultural treasures, remarkable buildings, attractive streets, and public spaces that are economic as well as social assets. They have begun to revive because our economy needs cities that work. We must encourage a change in urban attitudes so that towns and cities once again become attractive places to live, work, and socialize in.

A well-designed city demands a flexible structure and a clear articulation of public spaces that not only connects different communities to each other, but also links people to their homes, schools, workplaces, and basic social institutions. Most people would be prepared to walk five minutes to reach their neighbourhood shop, school, or local bus stop before resorting to the car. A successful urban district should sustain a range of commercial and social facilities, including civic space, leisure facilities, schools, and parks for tranquil recreation. Urban design determines the shape of the streets and public spaces that make up our urban form. Architecture forms a vital component within this framework, determining the shape, function, and aesthetic quality of the buildings that make up our collective urban experience. By weaving together the natural with the man-made, architecture, landscape, and urban design establish a balance between people and their environment.

People respond to beauty in cities. They choose to walk from one destination to another along favoured routes. Good design should provide a stimulus to the senses through choice of materials, architectural form, and landscaping. The long-term strategy for the governance and maintenance of urban fabric is as important as originality of design.

A tree-lined street with friendly neighbours, good corner shops, a well-cared-for local park, and a public library: these are the benefits of city living and they can help create a sense of closeness and community. *Coronation Street* is not just fiction: it reflects the great potential of the street and neighbourhood to support individual and collective life. People make cities, and cities make citizens. In public spaces, the harshness of city life can melt away in a reordering of the built and social environment. People can make them come to life as a melting-pot of ages, races, and backgrounds. Making cities work for all their citizens, rich and poor, is the challenge of the new urbanized millennium. With better education and fiscal and legal commitment, we can meet this challenge.

I am also calling on people in every street and neighbourhood to reclaim and stand up for their cities; to demand a better deal from their elected representatives; to renew and reassert their civic pride; and to work together to achieve the vision of 'Cities built for People'. This is no utopian vision. Cities that are beautiful, safe, and just are within our grasp.

6

Introduction to Patrick Declerck

Maria Kaika

A philosopher, ethnologist, and psychoanalyst practising in Paris, Patrick Declerck is also a sharp critic of social attitudes in the Western world towards poverty in general and towards homelessness in particular. Declerck possesses a curious distinction among his fellow intellectuals in France: his is the only citation index to rise as the temperature falls. This is because, as Declerck observes in his lecture, the French government mobilizes its action plan for the homeless only once the temperature has dropped below 2 degrees centigrade.

Declerck attacks this plan for establishing what he calls a 'thermal limit to the social contract'. This limit means that the predicament of those who are down and out in the streets of Paris appears unacceptable to the rest of society *only* when the temperature is low. At any other time, Parisian society and the French political establishment accept the suffering of the homeless as a 'necessary' evil. This acceptance, Declerck argues with passionate conviction, is part of the inner sadism with which mainstream Western societies treat poor and homeless people.

Declerck bases his convictions upon rigorous research and continuous practical experience. He worked with homeless people in Paris for fifteen years, went down and out with the homeless for periods over a number of years, and—most important of all—helped found, in 1986, the first counselling and medical treatment service for the homeless in France. His book *Les Naufragés* (The Shipwrecked) (2001) combines these various experiences in a rigorous study of the homeless of Paris. The work, which has had a considerable impact in France but has unfortunately not yet been translated into English, is a testimony of Declerck's experiences of living with the homeless, a narrative of their lives, and an account of the conversations he had with them. It is an effort to put homeless people and their plight 'on the map'. It goes beyond a rigorous ethnographic description of the homeless of Paris to offer an explanation of *how* these people come to exist in our cities and *why* they remain in this position for so many years.

Declerck's Oxford Amnesty Lecture, a synthesis of his argument in *Les Naufragés*, offers a highly provocative psycho-analytic interpretation and critique of social exclusion. It contends that long-term homelessness is a form of mental illness and that it should be treated as such. It also argues that our society does not simply fail to treat the homeless adequately, but on the contrary, that it punishes them. Declerck sees the 'structural inadequacy' of welfare provision for the homeless as a form of social sadism. For our society, he insists, hates those who live at its margins and willingly punishes those who mock everything that it holds dear.

This kind of social sadism towards the marginalized is not new to modern societies. One need only recall Malthus's *Essay on the Principle of Population* (1798) in which he argues for the gradual abolition of the Poor Laws in England because, in his view, they merely perpetuate poverty. It would be more interesting, however, to juxtapose Declerck's argument with another early analysis of the condition of the working class in England. Writing in 1845, Engels argued against Malthus that the existence of the urban poor, far from being undesirable to Western societies, is in fact a necessary condition for the efficient functioning of any capitalist economy. According to Engels, these people form a 'reserve army of unemployed workers' leading lives so miserable that they would take on any odd job, at any given moment and at very low wages, just to keep afloat. Their availability causes wages to be lowered, helping to raise the profits of industry, and promotes social discipline since those who hold jobs are under constant threat of being replaced.

However—and this is where Declerck's argument links in—the long-term homeless slip through the nets of job seeking and social discipline alike. Instead of performing their social function as part of the reserve army of workers, they opt out of this miserable fate and drift into a different sort of existence. Perhaps then—one might reply to Declerck—the social sadism with which our society treats the long-term homeless has to do less with them having what the majority of the population secretly desires (such as not having to be woken by an alarm clock every morning) and more to do with the fact that a market economy needs to whip such people into being ready at any given moment to pay their dues and return to a 'productive life'. It may be of course that both explanations are valid and constitute the Janus face of contemporary social sadism.

The symbolic place of the homeless—both in lived Hell (where they suffer the punishment we fear for not complying with the rules) and in lived Heaven (where they enjoy the 'freedom' we desire yet never dare to spell out or achieve)—is seductive. It can easily lead to a romanticized attitude towards homeless people. However, their 'Faustian deal', which offers an escape route from reality through mental illness, is too raw to lend itself to any form of romanticism. Patrick Declerck's deconstruction of the idea of a homeless community and his account of the misery and madness of the everyday lives of the homeless make this very clear. Their mockery of society's rules and expectations is too threatening for society to agree to accommodate their madness. There is no doubt that our urban Heaven needs to have an urban Hell lurking in its backyard, if for no other reason than that it has to define itself against its 'other'. But urban Heaven cannot bear to have urban Hell laughing in its face.

On the Necessary Suffering of the Homeless

Patrick Declerck

Cities are the birthplace of the social contract and of human rights. They are also the place in which homeless people can be seen every day, clinging on to life in the most appalling conditions. In other words, cities are the site of a deep division between a socialized majority and a desocialized minority. Far from being an unfortunate accident of urban life, this division is a structural necessity for cities in the so-called developed world. There are two main reasons for this division. The first is that cities offer the homeless an escape from the claustro-phobia they have experienced in close family ties and social networks while affording the largest concentration of people from which to beg. The second is that cities are the stage on which society chooses to display the price paid by those who do not accept—because they cannot—the obligations of social existence, in particular, the obligation to work. So cities are not only the birthplace of human rights; they also reveal the limits that society chooses to set on those rights.

I worked and lived with the homeless of Paris for fifteen years. I first came into contact with them as an ethnologist trying to make sense of the lives they lead. This attempt enabled me to share their lives in some degree: like an earlier urban ethnologist, the George Orwell of *Down and Out in Paris and London*,[1] I learnt what it is to beg, to be arrested by the police, and to sleep in shelters. I am also a psychoanalyst and in 1986, with the organization Médecins du Monde

(Doctors of the World), I opened the first counselling and medical services for the homeless in France. The years I spent working with the homeless raised questions that shake the fundamental concepts of psychiatry, medicine, sociology, and pyschoanalysis. I cannot hope to do justice to these questions in so short a space. But what I can offer, at the very least, is a better and deeper understanding of the suffering of the homeless and the almost unimaginable horror that surrounds their daily lives. By 'understanding', I mean a cognitive process at once rational and heartfelt, a mixture of comprehension and empathy. I hope also to convey the fact that the homeless deserve to be understood rather than ignored, patronized, or hated. For the horror of their situation is not unique to them; it is also ours. The plight of the homeless is compounded by the insidious sadism of a society—our society—that needs to punish those who live on its fringes and which, to this end, ensures that the health and welfare provisions made for the homeless are structurally inadequate. It is crucial to our understanding of the homeless, in other words, to see that their suffering is as necessary to us as it is to them.

This, I admit, is an unpleasant thought. Yet I have come to the conclusion that the way in which society systematically treats, or should I say mistreats, the people who live on its fringes—homeless people, prostitutes, and criminals—reveals the secret totalitarianism of the way in which we choose to live together. To my mind, the inescapable conclusion of the work I have done is that society, unwittingly but unerringly, sees to it that no viable existence is possible for those people who seem to mock normality, shun work, and enjoy idleness. Christianity and its lay versions speak of brotherly love and charity for all. But, despite this, homeless people are by and large harrassed, abandoned, and condemned to horrific suffering. How do we allow this to happen? Because, in a word, we hate them. We hate them because they refuse to work and because they seem to mock everything we hold dear: hope, self-betterment, personal relationships, pro-creation, bringing up children, and even simply getting up in the morning. They are dirty, smelly, incontinent, and unsoci-able, and as such they are a living insult to our aspirations and our narcissism. In my view, that is also precisely why they are so precious and so fascinating.

What exactly is 'homelessness'? One hears in the media that there has been an earthquake in Nicaragua and that two thousand people have been left 'homeless'. It is well known too that our streets are increasingly full of illegal economic migrants, poor people without the proper papers or a roof over their heads, but who are working to better themselves. These people are not desocialized: they are just poor. By 'homelessness', I mean neither the condition of people tem-porarily deprived of their homes nor that of people who aspire to a home and a normal life for themselves and their families. I mean chronic, long-term homelessness, the condi-tion of extreme desocialization into which some people drift and which they seem unable or unwilling ever to leave. Those affected include drinkers, drug users, and the mentally ill; many of the long-term homeless suffer from all these prob-lems. They were once called 'tramps', but we now prefer to use less openly pejorative terms. I think of them as 'the shipwrecked'. They seem to us to have made some kind of Faustian choice to live on the streets, to have settled in dys-topia forever, and to lead their entire lives in an existential unintelligibility. Those are the people I am talking about.

I started to work with them in 1982. By then, I had trained as a philosopher, and written a Master's thesis on the mystical aspects of Wittgenstein's *Tractatus Logico-Philosophicus* (1922). I found philosophy a lot of fun—or rather it was, like all abstruse occupations, both pleasurable and obscurely dissatisfying. In his *Pensées*, Pascal called them a *divertissement*, a term that covers both 'entertainment' and 'distraction' and refers to the forms of entertainment that people invent in order to distract themselves from the reality of suffering and ultimate death. I wanted to use philosophical anthropology to study that reality and I wanted to become more clinical in my approach. 'Clinical', a term that comes from the Greek word meaning 'bed', refers to what we observe and experience when we stand at the patient's bedside. That was what interested me.

I thought that I would start off by doing a doctorate in ethnology and working with the homeless. That didn't go very well, because to do a doctorate in ethnology you need to find an ethnological object of study out there 'in the field', and it turned out that the streets offered nothing of the kind. This was my first surprise. My colleagues in ethnology and I had worried about the trouble I would have in penetrating the milieu, in obtaining permission to hang around with the homeless, in being accepted by them. We thought we were dealing with an alternative society that had laws, chiefs, organizations, and symbols of its own; that as in all societies, there would be procedures of inclusion, doors to enter; and that this would be no easy task. But I soon discovered that there were no doors and no difficulty, since all one had to do was dress oddly (which is no problem for me anyway) and then simply venture on to the streets. Going out into the city, sitting down in a doorway, begging from passers-by, sharing a bottle of wine with the tramps, and observing their daily lives: all of this was immediately possible, indeed, it was easy. The truth is that nothingness has no doors; that one can indeed go through the looking-glass, but one ends up nowhere.

There was no alternative society or organizing group. What I discovered instead was nothing more than a loose collection of individuals, broken men and women, who were desperately trying to survive hour by hour. Most were alcoholics also involved in some form of substance abuse. I worked sub-sequently at a hospital, located in Nanterre on the outskirts of Paris, which had been a poorhouse and specialized in the treatment of homeless people. There a doctor colleague of mine and I calculated that 95 per cent of the patients we saw consumed the equivalent in alcohol of between 4 and 5 litres of wine per day. Add to that the substance abuse, medication, malnutrition, and the exhaustion of living in the street, and you have a cocktail that leaves people in a state bordering on unconsciousness. Each of the homeless people I met seemed to live in an enclosed mental world which was remarkably poor, depleted, and repetitive. It is hardly surprising that they didn't give a damn who I was, what I was doing there, or what my story was.

I, of course, was more able to take an interest in them and in their stories. Anthropology, whatever its limitations, springs from the worthy impulse to observe the experience of others, to make sense of that experience in its own terms, to add as it were one's pound of flesh to the balance. To observe begging and to beg oneself are very different propositions, and for that reason, I decided to do the latter—a technique known as 'participant observation'—as well as the former. It changed my perspective entirely. It is difficult to find adequate words for the weight of contempt that one experiences, to describe what it feels like to be spat on and to have people call you names. Sleeping rough—if you manage to sleep at all, because the experience is terrifying—means suffering the proximity of rats, the indignity of being peed upon by dogs, and the real and present threat of being attacked by humans. It is like living in *A Clockwork Orange*. Homeless women are constantly prey to the danger of rape, and to lessen that danger they flee headlong into their madness and psychosis, becoming the terrifying and toothless witches that we see on the streets. Dramatic as it may seem, this brief phenomenology of being down and out is perfectly banal, and constitutes the homeless person's daily life. Imagine for a moment, if you will, the shame and the sheer physical difficulty of bringing oneself to defecate in public. For homeless people, this is a daily occurrence: public toilets are not all that common, and if you're too dirty, they won't let you into a pub or café. Homeless people do develop friendships with one another. Some form couples. Single men often sleep in groups, mainly as a defensive measure, to lessen the chance that they might be attacked. All of these relationships are very unstable, as one would expect of relationships between people who are drunk most of the time: theft is common, as are sexual aggression and violence. Street life is essentially an experience of profound boredom shot through with moments of terror and punctuated by the chaos of drunken people fighting, crying, getting back together, and fighting again.

It is extremely hard to fathom the depth of suffering that these people endure. And yet they prove extremely hard to treat. They are a group of people that the prevalent discourse of social exclusion fails singularly to comprehend. Because after all, if these people were the helpless victims of social 'exclusion', one would suppose that it would be relatively easy for society to recognize that and consequently include them. One would need only to open doors for them—provide them with a social security number, the chance to work, and a place to live—and they would get better.

But this is not the case. Homeless people confront us with the scandal of extreme masochism. Theirs, it seems, is the perverseness of those who prefer the worst. It is as if they actually wanted to suffer. We are reminded here of Herman Melville's short story 'Bartleby'.[2] Bartleby, a solicitor's copyist, goes into the office one day in the normal way. But when his superiors give him some work to do, he says, very politely: 'I would prefer not to.' This phrase, having made its sudden and untimely intervention, eats into his life like a cancer: 'I would prefer not to' becomes all that he has to say as, progressively, he shies away from all forms of activity. Ultimately he dies, anorexic and in a state of total self-abandonment, in the poorhouse. 'I would prefer not to.' The greatness of Melville's story is that he offers no psycho-babble, no insight, not the first inkling of an explanation of that famous phrase. It is a version of what psychoanalysts call 'the negative', by which they mean the vertigo of human life, its dark side.[3] Chronic homelessness cannot be reduced to poverty, dereliction, or social exclusion. It is the madness of poverty, the madness of dereliction, the madness of social exclusion. It is, in a word, madness. And like all mad people, homeless people are very precious, both for the questions they raise and for the mockery they make of our aspirations. They show us the dark side of ourselves, the one that we do not want to be reminded of, the negative within us.

We hate their guts for it. That is why we devise a system of social health and medicine for the homeless, a whole paraphernalia of help provision, that is and is intended to be structurally inadequate. Let me quote, as one example of this, a document I have obtained from the Head Office of the

Department for Social and Sanitary Affairs in Paris. This document defines the conditions under which emergency shelters for the homeless are to be opened in the winter months. The conditions are as follows: 'The night temperature must attain minus 2 degrees centigrade, and the day temperature must stay beneath plus 2 degrees centigrade, unless there are aggravating factors such as snow, rain, and wind. Weather forecasts for the next few days and nights must also be taken into account.'[4] This is a fundamental anthropological document because it candidly sets what might be called a thermal limit to the social contract. It is paradigmatic of what I am trying to argue. What is this document about? Presumably, if emergency shelters are to be opened at all during cold weather, their aim must be to prevent the onset of hypothermia in homeless people. Everybody knows that the body temperature of humans is 36.8 degrees centigrade. But the document speaks of average outside temperatures of zero degrees. Now what has 36.8 degrees centigrade in common with the freezing point of a substance called H_2O?

The answer is: nothing at all. Anyone who has done even a little medicine knows that for the ill-dressed, undernourished, and exhausted, hypothermia is a very real possibility from around 15 or 16 degrees centigrade downwards. So this document has nothing whatsoever to do with hypothermia. It has to do with us: it is an attempt to calculate what the well-dressed, well-fed, and well-rested perceive as cold weather. If you die of hypothermia on a street corner some day when the average temperature is around plus 4 degrees centigrade, it will be a matter of some regret to the Parisian authorities. But they will not really consider it their problem. Certainly they would not regard it as justifying the mobilization of their resources or the opening of their emergency shelters. It is really only when *the rest of us* start to feel the cold—as we go from our cars to our houses—that society and its leaders start trying to prevent homeless people from freezing to death. This is a fundamental problem. It suggests that we are able to care for these people only in so far as we can identify with them. If we cannot identify with them—simply because we feel warm or they seem too strange and unintelligible—then disregard and hatred insidiously set in.

There are numerous examples of this tendency. There is a very worthy institution in France called *Les Restaurants du cœur* (Restaurants of the Heart). (As an aside, allow me to draw your attention to the fact that the whole field of provision for the homeless is permeated with saccharine sentiments of the kind expressed in this name. It would be refreshing to hear of 'Restaurants of the Spleen'. But I suppose one cannot hope for too much.) The Restaurants of the Heart are open six months each year and last year distributed 60 million meals to homeless people. My question is simple: what happened to the other six months and the other 60 million meals? There is no logic to this. If we recognize the need to give free food to destitute people, then we must also recognize that for six months in every year we are starving them. But we seem to think that feeding them for half the year is enough.

That thought reveals an immense contempt. It also reveals, to my mind, the unconscious desire of mainstream society to maintain a degree of visible suffering in the lives of the homeless. Homelessness is at some level seductive to us all and for that reason it is dangerous. Like all madness, it offers the mirage of a way out and an illusion of escape from the demands of reality, and those demands are something the rest of us have to suffer. Thus there is something seductive, vertiginous, danger-ous about the thought of homelessness. If the lives of the homeless were made too comfortable, we worry that we might all be seduced into letting go or saying, like Bartleby, 'I would prefer not to.' Those moments of regression, when the alarm clock goes off and we turn it off with a lazy hand or put a pillow over our heads, might spread throughout our lives: we might turn our backs on reality.

Regression is a seductive possibility for everyone. And the homeless are past masters of regression. Most have regressed to the level of infants: medical care of them often poses problems similar to those faced in paedopsychiatry. 'His Majesty the Baby', said Freud, to explain the demands that children place upon their parents. 'His Majesty the Tramp' is the appropriate phrase here. I do not mean to suggest that the lives of all homeless people can never improve. But the key to improvement, when it happens, is the development of a 'transferential' relationship with someone else, in other words, one through which the unconscious fantasies, demands, and needs of the homeless person can be expressed and met. This is, in psychological terms, a surrogate mother–child bond. All too often, of course, homeless people fail to sustain transferential relationships. They exhibit what I call the 'syndrome of desocialization': a psychopathological incapacity to maintain relationships with society at large, with the demands of everyday reality, with others; but, first and foremost, with themselves.

Chronic homelessness, like all symptoms, is a compromise. The compromise is in this case between life and fantasies of implosion, psychotic breakdown, suicide, and murder. What allows the homeless to maintain this compromise is the hustle and bustle, the constant activity, the fight for survival of their everyday lives. The inadequacy of our provisions—the soup kitchen to which one can go today but not tomorrow, the emergency shelter in which one can spend only two consecutive nights before having to move on—condemns the homeless to a constant game of musical chairs. It is a strange and paradoxical fact that, even though they seem to avoid all kinds of obligation, they live in a manner that obliges them to spend immense energy simply on surviving the next few hours. The constant fight for survival is in its own way a kind of grim *divertissement*: it keeps at bay the self-destructive fantasies and anguish that come from within. Often it is when life ostensibly improves for homeless people, when they are given a hotel room in which to stay for a reasonable period of time, that the monsters come out.

There is nothing worse for such people than to be alone in the dark. When I was working for the Doctors of the World organization, I had a patient staying in a hotel room who came to see me each day. One day he phoned to tell me that he could not leave his room; he was too frightened; would I come to his hotel for our daily session? He was not a psychotic patient, but when I arrived he was sitting in bed with the covers over his head, unable to move. He could not leave his room because he was worried he would go into the underground and throw himself in front of an oncoming train. He could not get up because that would mean shaving in front of the mirror and he was terrified of cutting his throat. He was, clearly, in mortal fear of his own razor. So we had our daily session in the usual way, except that he lay in bed and I sat beside him on a chair. At the end of the session I took him around his room. We opened the one cupboard in the room, looked under the bed, went in and out of the bathroom, and when we had done so he said he felt better. It was a case of calming his fears, for his monsters were out and he needed me to play the role of the exorcist. I looked after this patient of mine as though I were a parent to a small child. Much of the treatment in this field, as I said earlier, is no more than applied paedopsychiatry.

No sooner do most homeless people find themselves in a transferential relationship of this kind with a carer than they fall back into their old ways. Why do such relapses occur? The answer is that the one thing homeless people have in common is terrible relationships with their mothers. Psychoanalysis talks of the need for what Winnicott called a 'good enough' structure in a life: a good enough relationship with one's mother is a precondition of maintaining a good enough relationship with oneself, one's fears, and fantasies.[5] Unfortunately, for homeless people, things have gone very badly from a very early age. They have suffered abandonment, bereavement, alcoholism, threats of violence and incest; they have become delinquent, criminal, and dependent on alcohol and other drugs. They have been set aside; or alternatively—and they cannot decide which way round it is—they have set themselves aside.

What causes the marginalization of the homeless? This question inevitably raises the issue of responsibility and guilt. Questions of causes or origins always seem to become questions of guilt when it comes to the homeless. We want to know whose fault it is that these people live as they do: are they victims, or are they perverts who have expressed their free will in a disgusting negative choice? Free will, in my view, plays no part in the condition of homelessness; in fact, the whole concept of will is no more than a tool of moral oppression, a fantasy of normality. The further one looks into mental pathology, the more empty of meaning the concept of will becomes. Schopenhauer, like Freud, saw this long ago.[6] And yet those in the field of social work and medicine constantly function as if free will were a reality. Several facts are well known about alcoholic addiction: one is that that the treatment often takes up to seven or eight years to work; another is that long-term abstinence is achieved in no more than about a third of cases. Despite this, homeless people—the great majority of whom are addicted to alcohol—are at best offered a six-month stay in an institution, which can be renewed once if they keep their noses clean. When they arrive, they are greeted with the following speech: 'We know that you're an alcoholic and that you are suffering from depression and we can offer you treatment. For this treatment to work, you must get up at seven o'clock each morning, take a shower, have breakfast, go to work; you will come back from work at six, have dinner at six-thirty, and go to bed after watching television game shows for about an hour and a half. If you do that for six months, we may give you another six months, and then you will be cured.' This is not even a caricature of the procedure; it is simply what happens. The disregard shown for psychiatry, sociology, and psychoanalysis is complete. It is a paradoxical kind of treatment in which one begins by asking the patients to give up all their symptoms. Then we hold seminars on why these apparently unintelligible perverts are not getting any better.

The relapses of homeless people, though accepted in conventional medicine in general, are rarely tolerated by institutions. There they are viewed as insulting transgressions. 'So you've got drunk AGAIN,' is the common reaction: 'Do it one more time and I'll kick you out.' When 95 per cent of one's clientele is composed of alcoholics, one ought to expect them to get drunk once in a while. Such relapses, which are bound to happen, are nevertheless regarded as deliberately destructive acts on the part of the patients, who quickly find themselves back on the streets again, paying for the same problems a second time. That, once again, is sadistic.

A major problem here is that the system refuses to acknowledge the existence of chronic illness. Some people, for unaccountable and extremely complex reasons, will in effect be lifelong victims of their own incapacity to meet the minimum demands of normality. To our democratic 'ideology', by which I mean the realm of existence in which we accept or reject images of behaviour and belief, the notion of 'chronicity' is extremely unsettling because it implies that there are irreducible differences between people. We make a point of treating all people as equals, which is fine; but we also treat them as interchangeable, which is false. We do so because we refuse to accept, out of self-defence, the fundamentally chronic nature of madness. It is of course the mad themselves who are made to pay the cost of that refusal. Society responds to the demands and needs of its lifelong incapacitated members by judging that they had better run the risk of regrettable accidents such as rape, or death from hypothermia, than be accepted for who they are. It would be too threatening to our society if the homeless were allowed decent living conditions; we would rather they suffered.

Of course, it does not have to be this way. It seems after all that, despite the best efforts of current medical research, the mortality rate is set to remain hovering on the verge of 100 per cent at least for the foreseeable future. Yet no one claims that we should disband the medical profession, close all the hospitals, and abolish social security simply because we are all going to die. Something similar could be said of the homeless: most will never be cured because, for most, there is no cure; but that is no reason why we should make them suffer. It is time we started to treat the homeless people on the streets of our cities with decency. To do so means admitting the responsibility that society has towards its members who are chronically incapable of functioning in a normal manner. It means, in effect, rethinking the boundaries of the social contract.

I am often accused of being 'pessimistic' about the suffering of the homeless. I do not know what that means. Wittgenstein, at the very beginning of the *Tractatus*, says: 'The world is all that is the case. The world is the totality of facts, not of things.'[7] That is true. But most people refuse to look at all the facts. I had a patient once whose name was L'Angoisse (Anguish). L'Angoisse had an ulcer that had eaten away most of his skin between his knee and his ankle. He had to be hospitalized on several occasions. When he came to our medical services, he was invariably dirty and his ulcer was infested with maggots. The doctor used to say to him: 'Why don't you try and keep the flies off your ulcer? The flies lay eggs, and the eggs become maggots.' L'Angoisse replied that he did not believe him. So one day the doctor decided to show him that what he had said was true. He took some of the maggots out of the patient's ulcer, put them in a box, and a few days later the maggots became flies. On seeing this, L'Angoisse said to the doctor: 'Those are my flies, aren't they? Would you keep them safe for me?' We duly preserved them in alcohol. In the course of the following weeks, L'Angoisse visited the hospital again and again, and each time he said to us: 'Would you let me play with my children?'

This is a horrendous story. It is indecent, degrading, and thoroughly mad. But it also carries the distant echo of a fundamental human urge: to live on after one's own death, to give life to something else, be it dead flies. It is only by understanding the fundamental humanity that we share with chronically homeless people that we can hope to give them the respect they deserve. The responsibility is ours alone. It means saying of L'Angoisse what Prospero says of Caliban: 'This thing of darkness I acknowledge mine.'[8]

Part II
Responses

7

Who Should Foot the Bill?

Michael B. Likosky

Should the urban poor be asked to pay their way out of poverty? Should transnational corporations be invited to profit from the plight of the urban poor? I fear that, if we use privatization to solve urban poverty, then we are answering 'yes' to these questions. In his impassioned and challenging contribution to this collection, World Bank President James Wolfensohn describes the World Bank's Cities Without Slums action plan. This plan is in the process of upgrading infrastructures and services in urban slums globally. However, this plan and others like it seek in part to solve urban poverty by using the specific privatization technique of the public–private partnership. By harnessing the power of transnational corporations to solve urban poverty, such partnerships demand that the poor pay private companies for what should be their birthright: a basic social and economic infrastructure.

In this response, I'd like to highlight three pieces for special attention: the lectures by Stuart Hall, David Harvey, and James Wolfensohn. Hall and Harvey's account of the relationship between globalization, privatization, and urban poverty is very different from that offered by Wolfensohn. For Hall and Harvey, globalization impoverishes, while for Wolfensohn it is the key to solving the problem of urban poverty. With minor qualifications I will side with Hall and Harvey and argue that, while Wolfensohn's position has important merits, it should be modified in significant ways.

It seems to me that many of the problems of urban poverty are caused by globalization. The bill for eradicating urban poverty should be handed to the beneficiaries of globalization, not to its victims.

I'll start by fleshing out a recurring theme in all three chapters, the privatization of our cities, before giving some sense of how the privatization of urban infrastructure has come about over the last twenty-five or so years. Then I'll turn to the lectures by Hall, Harvey, and Wolfensohn.

The Privatization of Urban Infrastructure

The privatization of urban infrastructures started in the late 1970s in the United Kingdom. It was part of what Stuart Hall in his contribution refers to as 'the privatization of public goods'. Before this, urban infrastructures were run by state corporations and were often financed from the government budget or—in developing countries—by the World Bank through direct grants. However, in a movement led by Margaret Thatcher and closely followed by Ronald Reagan, infrastructures were systematically transferred to private corporations. This movement quickly spread from its trans-Atlantic cradle to almost every corner of the globe.[1]

Every continent and most cities have been touched by privatization. Governments everywhere did not simply wake up having seen the light. Instead, privatization was hawked by such international organizations as the World Bank, the International Monetary Fund, and the United Nations Industrial Development Organization. These were not the only salespeople. The governments of fully industrialized countries have also pushed privatization techniques. The US government has helped things along through aid programmes and the European Union has encouraged its new members to adopt the privatization approach.[2]

Why were fully industrialized governments so intent on spreading the gospel of privatization? Many reasons are adduced including the inefficiency of state-owned infrastructure companies and the inability of Third World states affected by the debt crisis to pay for new infrastructures. At the same time, we should not forget that many of the most powerful transnational infrastructure companies hail from fully industrialized states. So a government victory abroad for privatization often meant a new business opportunity opened up at home for its corporate nationals. These companies were not simply invited to operate pre-existing infrastructures. Often they were granted the right to build new large-scale and expensive infrastructures.

'Privatization' suggests that a transfer of public goods into private hands has occurred. The term is, however, a misnomer, since 'privatization' in effect means that corporations will be invited into the infrastructure game as major players, poised to profit.[3] These corporations will be able to count on the government to help them realize their profit potential. It is really a public–private partnership. Let me give an example. One of the most popular legal techniques for putting privatization into practice is the 'build-operate-transfer' (BOT) contract. BOT contracts are wildly popular: the Channel Tunnel connecting Paris and London was carried out with the BOT technique; roads are built in Asia with them; they are used in many other areas. As the term implies, under a BOT contract, a private company 'builds' the infrastructure; it 'operates' the infrastructure to recoup its sunk costs and to garner a profit; it then 'transfers' ownership of the infrastructure to the government. So under this technique, the ultimate effect of privatization is that the infrastructure is bestowed on the state.[4]

Not only is the state the ultimate owner of many urban infrastructure projects, but governments are involved in pushing privatization in a whole host of other ways. For instance, fully industrialized countries often subsidize infrastructure nationals doing business abroad through their export credit agencies. These are government agencies established to promote foreign commerce by corporate nationals through subsidies of various sorts. The host government of an infrastructure company might also give its guarantee to the international investment banks underwriting company projects. They may do this by guaranteeing that if its citizens are unable to pay their electricity or water bills to the foreign corporation, then the government will step in and pay them. Governments may also quash political protests that target transnational privatized infrastructure projects.

Privatization can be seen in further fundamental respects to be underpinned by ongoing government and intergovernmental support. We see this in the endowing of corporations with legal personality (the public law foundations of the commercial order), the new laws concerning property rights, and in the general trend within the US and in international law towards the promoting of corporate rights over human rights.

How do the urban poor figure in all of this? What happens when privatization sets its sights on urban poverty and does so through specific legal techniques? Broadly speaking, when a transnational water company lays pipes, it recoups its sunk costs by charging users. It may take decades for sunk costs to be recouped and for a profit to be captured. The cost incurred by the water company in laying its infrastructure is recouped by charging water users each time they turn on their taps. The meter starts running. This is fine when the drinkers and bathers earn a decent income for a hard day's work. But what is to be done when their income is substandard, the work often gruelling, and the water sometimes not drinkable?

Privatization and the City: Problem or Solution?

This is how globalization takes root in our cities through privatization. In their contributions to this volume, Hall, Harvey, and Wolfensohn all draw connections between globalization, privatization, and urban poverty. But the connections they draw vary widely. Hall and Harvey are on one side of the fence; Wolfensohn is on the other. From where Hall and Harvey stand, privatization is the cause of poverty, while on Wolfensohn's side it is the solution to poverty.

Hall and Harvey are sharply critical of the policies of the international institutions and powerful states that drive globalization. One of the major international organizations singled out for criticism is the World Bank at whose helm Wolfensohn stands. Hall sets his sights on the Bank, along with the International Monetary Fund and the World Trade Organization. Harvey shares Hall's target and asks: 'Can social injustice—as signalled by the ghastly poverty that haunts the world more generally but which is most concentrated in cities—be eradicated, as the World Bank and the International Monetary Fund insist, by the proper application of some version of free market capitalism?' These institutions push a form of 'global governance' of which the privatizations discussed above are one pillar.

The apparently benign term 'the global', for Hall, masks a nefarious process whose engine is the 'hegemonic deregulating, free-market, privatizing, neo-liberal economic regime'. This is a mouthful, but I think it's accurate. This regime takes many forms around the world and includes the US 'Washington Consensus' and current New Labour policies in the UK. It is advanced by an 'unholy alliance' of fully industrialized governments and 'global corporate forces' in collusion with indigenous elites. When it comes to the problems of the 'marginalized poor', Hall is dubious about the ability of the 'neo-liberal "world system" ' to make everything all right. Harvey is pointed, arguing: 'the liberalization not only of trade but of financial markets across the globe has unleashed a storm of speculative powers in which predatory capital has plundered the world to the detriment of all else.'

Harvey sees the privatization of basic urban infrastructures, goods, and services as destroying common property rights by the 'privatization and commodification of all things' that 'are necessary preconditions for capital accumulation to proceed'. He notes that infrastructures such as education, health care, water, and sanitation have all been 'privatized and brought within the dominant regime of rights favourable to the circulation and accumulation of capital'. Here, the poor are dispossessed of their right to a basic social and economic infrastructure. It is this 'accumulation by dispossession' which Harvey argues is a 'dominant motif' of our present predicament.

Unlike many who see the state as being brushed aside by globalization, Hall makes it clear that the state continues to be a mover and shaker. This point is reinforced by the discussion above of the privatization of infrastructures globally—the public–private partnership approach. Privatization does not mean corporations displacing governments, but instead governments and companies joining together in partnership to push a common agenda. This might not be an agenda of great popular appeal. Many would say, indeed, that it runs roughshod over our cities and the urban poor.

It is the impact of globalization on the poor of our cities that concerns Hall. Cities are deeply divided places and globalization affects people differently depending upon their wealth and status. Hall reminds us of the salient urban divisions which are 'by class and wealth, by rights to and over property, by occupation and use, by lifestyle and culture, by race and nationality, ethnicity and religion, and by gender and sexuality'. These are the same cities that Harvey describes: 'migratory streams from everywhere; business elites in motion; professors and consultants on the wing; diasporas networking across borders (often clandestinely); illegals and *sans papiers*; the dispossessed that sleep in doorways and beg on the street in the midst of the greatest affluence; ethnic and religious cleansings; strange mixings and odd confrontations'. For Harvey, 'the so-called "global" cities are divided socially between the financial elites and the great swathes of lower paid service workers melding into the marginalized and unemployed'. These divisions are expressed in 'the city's cartography' in which rich and poor occupy different areas of the city. Hall argues that globalization has reinforced the power position of the rich, while exploiting and reproducing 'divisions and differences within the global city'. Although globalization promises a levelling of the global playing field, 'resources, opportunities, and life-chances are not being levelled or equalized across the globe or within the city'. People are being brought into the global system differently. It matters if one is a supermarket executive or a worker picking runner beans in East Africa. For Hall, anti-poverty initiatives have 'comprehensively failed to deliver'. These initiatives are 'designed to make the poor complicit with their global fate'.

Such a claim must be taken seriously, particularly as we turn to the Wolfensohn argument. While Harvey believes that 'basic needs, like clean water, are denied to those who do not have the ability to pay', Wolfensohn contends that privatization can rid our urban centres of poverty. Basic services can be delivered to all through public–private partnerships. The purchasing power of the poor is, according to Wolfensohn, grossly underestimated.

Wolfensohn describes how the World Bank has set out to end urban poverty through its Cities Without Slums action plan. The Bank and others, according to Wolfensohn, have recognized that the problem of poverty must be faced because the inexorable march of globalization has made clear to all that 'in the areas of health, education, communications, finance, migration, and so many others, we all belong, for better or worse, to one world'. For Wolfensohn, globalization is not the cause of poverty, but rather the route out of it.

To solve the problem of poverty, Wolfensohn argues we must adopt a new paradigm of development, one premised upon partnership. These public–private partnerships include 'a coalition of forces', 'institutions such as the [World] Bank and bi-lateral institutions [. . .], civil society, the private sector, [. . .] poor people themselves exercising their rights as full citizens', and faith-based organizations. This cadre is brought together, in partnership, to solve the problem of urban poverty. The World Bank seeks to put this approach into practice in urban centres through its Cities Without Slums action plan.

The World Bank, together with UN-HABITAT, created the Cities Alliance, an urban development coalition. This Alliance in turn put together the Cities Without Slums action plan. Through the action plan, the World Bank seeks to deliver basic social and economic infrastructure to urban slums. This infrastructure includes such things as 'water, sanitation, waste collection, storm drainage, street lighting, paved footpaths, and roads for emergency access'. The rationale for the Cities Without Slums action plan is not limited to the demands of social justice. The plan has attracted the support of urban politicians. It has done so by appealing to their rational self-interest rather than to their altruism alone. This boils down to the difficulty of attracting investment into cities blighted by urban poverty. The walls that have been erected between urban slums and affluence 'block incoming investment as well as greater social cohesion' and are therefore bad for the bottom line. Increasing incoming investment to affluent communities might have been the initial goal of mayors. Now, through initiatives like the Cities Without Slums plan, the private sector is being wooed into fighting poverty. According to Wolfensohn, private companies are more important than international aid agencies in combating urban poverty. Alongside these private companies, the financial investment of slum dwellers is also necessary. In involving slum dwellers in this initiative, the aim is to allow them 'to contribute socially and economically' to urban development.

It is this mobilizing of the poor to finance their basic social and economic infrastructure that worries me. While the Cities Without Slums initiative has an unequivocally large number of successes, it concerns me to hear Wolfensohn talk of mobilizing the economic resources of the poor to finance their economic and social infrastructure. He tells us that poor people invest seven dollars of their own money for every dollar invested by government. This, he says, 'explodes the myth that people in poverty have no money'. I worry that this is an open invitation to private infrastructure companies to exploit the urban poor, making them foot the bill for the problems caused by globalization.

In this respect, I agree with Hall and Harvey that globalization itself has produced poverty. While Wolfensohn sees no correlation between the spread of globalization and the spread of urban poverty, Hall and Harvey see causation. If globalization has underdeveloped urban infrastructures for the poor, should the poor then be asked to fuel globalization in their attempt to escape from urban poverty?

Wolfensohn tells a story about how the World Bank built basic infrastructure—a water and sewerage system—in a *favela* in Rio de Janeiro. He speaks of the genuine excitement of a woman in Rio who was able to enjoy the benefits of paying for water. It seems that the receipt of payment, which included her name and address, meant that she could secure a bank loan. She finally had a document confirming her residence. Paying for water meant much more than drinking and bathing: it unlocked the ability to be an economic citizen. While this is a success story, I wonder if there is no other way of encouraging banks to loan money to the urban poor besides asking the poor to pay their way out of poverty.

We must acknowledge that initiatives such as Cities Without Slums are not just about paving the way for private capital to exploit the urban poor. Companies are not involved in all aspects of these initiatives. Nevertheless, it is important to be attuned to how companies do get involved in things. And, when they are involved, what form does their involvement take? Who pays whom for the social and economic infrastructure of our urban slums? Is the infrastructure of the poor subsidized to the extent that we subsidize the infrastructure of our corporations?

It is for these reasons that, despite the important successes of the Cities Without Slums plan, I take issue with it. In doing so, I incline more to the positions taken by Hall and Harvey. Globalization and its agent, privatization, are the problem. Should we roll back privatization as suggested by Harvey? Perhaps. Should the right to basic social and economic infrastructure derive, as Harvey suggests, from a 'right to adequate life chances for all, to elementary material supports'? Yes.

Realizing a Right to the City through Basic Infrastructure

To put these rights into practice, urban social movements must have concrete targets and tangible ideas for how society will be remodelled if they are successful. This will ensure that 'positive outcomes rather than a descent into endless violence', as Harvey puts it, will ensue. The Cities Without Slums plan is not beyond repair. But if it is to become a genuinely equitable plan, it must be refashioned. I doubt that this will be done unless social movements target it.

One way that the Cities Without Slums plan could be reworked would be to harness the power of private capital differently. Private companies are undoubtedly the primary repositories of infrastructure-building expertise. They must be at the table. But it must be a table and not a trough. The working poor should not need to pay their way out of poverty in order to profit members of the very corporate class that is in part responsible for their poverty in the first place. Profit margins must be conservatively determined. And rather than charge the working poor for using infrastructures, the state (or foreign aid) should pay for the infrastructures of the urban poor.

Under privatization, states do not have to pay out of their budgets for infrastructures to be built. Instead, the cost of infrastructure is put on the shoulders of its users. The person who turns on the tap pays the water company. This is appealing to governments who are no longer responsible for providing basic infrastructure to its citizenry. It is less appealing to the working poor.

Governments have a responsibility to make sure that their citizenry can realize their basic human rights. A properly functioning urban infrastructure is essential here. To fulfil their responsibilities, governments should pay the infrastructure charges for the urban poor. This would not be an immediate strain on government budgets if incremental payments were stretched over decades. The cost could be covered through progressive taxation by governments. As taxpayers, many working poor will pay some of this cost. Perhaps if basic infrastructure is guaranteed by the state, we will be one step closer to allowing the working poor to exercise the 'right to the city' for which David Harvey makes such an eloquent case.

8

Looking on the Bright Side

Peter Hall

Responding is always an invidious business: unless you are in total empathy and sympathy with the viewpoint of the author, you run the risk of appearing simply churlish and grumpy. Of course, unless you believe, like the postmodernists, that there is no such thing as an objective statement, it is always possible to have arguments about the empirical truth, or otherwise, of what someone has written. But many pieces of writing are not like that: they represent what could be called a moral ordering of the world, with which you can agree or disagree according to your own such notions. And that is certainly true of the six lectures in this volume. How, writing for a volume in support of Amnesty International, could it be otherwise?

Take two of the lectures, which conceptually belong together almost like peas in a pod, those by Stuart Hall and David Harvey. They are perhaps the best-known British Marxist intellectuals, even though David Harvey now teaches in the United States. And they would deserve that appellation even if they were not occupying a lonely niche, since they are among the very few unapologetic Marxists left.

Stuart Hall emphasizes three key features driving change in our urban world: the uneven transition to a post-industrial economy and society, globalization, and migration. He asks:

What are the chances that we can construct in our cities shared, diverse, just, more inclusive, and egalitarian forms of common life, guaranteeing the full rights of democratic citizenship and participation to all on the basis of equality, whilst respecting the differences that inevitably come about when peoples of different religions, cultures, histories, languages, and traditions are obliged to live together in the same shared space?

This is a good question. But, if you know anything about writings in this tradition, you will know the answer in advance: 'The promises designed to make the poor complicit with their global fate—rising living standards, a more equal distribution of goods and life chances, an opportunity to compete on equal terms with the developed world, a fairer share of the world's wealth—have comprehensively failed to be delivered.'

There isn't much empirical evidence presented in support. Now it is true, and generally accepted, that in British and American cities (though not nearly to the same extent in other European cities) income inequality has increased over the past quarter century—almost exclusively because the rich have been getting much richer. And it is also true that by some measures international differences have been growing, though a lot depends on the precise measure you use. It would take a book to dissect this evidence fully, but you could reach an entirely different conclusion: internationally, that a whole series of examples (the Pacific Asian tiger economies, now joined by China) have indeed shown how to lift the great majority of their people rapidly out of poverty, and that others (notably India) now seem to be going in the same direction; that, within the UK, almost everyone has got richer but some have got much richer than others, because they possess what the economists call specific kinds of human capital which it is possible to acquire through education and training.

But Hall doesn't stop there, because in his view almost everything in our cities is in a state of progressive social disintegration. We have:

the long drift towards ethnic segregation in neighbourhood housing and in schools, a breakdown in communication between groups, the rivalry over scarce urban regeneration funding and poor local services [. . .] deepened by the fear of difference and change, the hatred stimulated by racism, the growth in Islamophobia, and a general failure of political leadership [. . .] The White working class [. . .] are open to the seductions of racially activist minority parties such as the National Front and the British National Party.

This doesn't sound much like the piece of a British city I happen to know, which is London's East End, peopled by one of the largest Islamic populations in Britain. That problems exist here, no one would deny: the community remains very poor; some, not all, of the Bengali young men are unwilling to follow their fathers into traditional occupations, are not making it through the school system, and are falling into drug-related crime; some of them are now starting to behave in a militant and racist manner towards whites; the white working class resent them because they think they are exploiting the welfare system. But there happens to be a lot of good news too, chiefly the performance of the girls who are raising themselves through education into the professional middle class and also into emancipation. Yet we don't hear any of the good news—only the bad.

What further emerges is that Hall cordially dislikes the new world of the 'new rich—the self-made tycoons, the celebrities and the new "flashocracy"—for whom key sites in the city are stage, playground, and photo-opportunity', of the 'creatives' who service this corporate and celebrity world, 'very different in background and in attitudes to the older professional and managerial middle-classes', who 'are the pioneers of an intense, designer-shaped, global consumerism, the avid readers of upmarket style mags and celebrity supplements and, culturally, exquisitely attuned to every minor shift or wobble in global postmodern taste-and design'. Well, this (non-related) Hall doesn't like much of it either. But that's just sour grapes on the part of a couple of semi-superannuated academics, I suspect. What Hall really dislikes is that they're young, rich, and having fun.

But he objects also to a side-effect: that the rest of us are pushed away from the 'trendified' city centres into places, 'typically areas of high and multiple disadvantage, with poor schools, forbidding estates, run-down or boarded-up high streets, high crime and drug rates, and drab terraces, [. . .] often of a dilapidated kind, poorly serviced and grim in terms of the conditions of life they offer'. Well, again, I don't know where he's been. I've recently walked a lot of those London streets for a book I'm doing, and I find them just fine: they're places that combine upward middle-class aspiration and enormous cultural vibrancy. Further, they tend to be ethnically and culturally mixed: with some exceptions (such as those Bengali young men), Londoners of all colours, creeds, and styles are living together with less tension and more enjoyment than in almost any other city on earth. Hall actually gets around to admitting this to be the case in 'some largely black areas in South London and elsewhere'; I believe that it goes a lot wider. But elsewhere, he asserts, 'the local populations—young and old—have fallen apart into a silent but sullen separateness, a hostile, mutual defensiveness'. Again, one would love to know where, or whom, he's actually talking about. It's true that in some parts of London, where new groups are moving into areas traditionally occupied by other groups, there's defensiveness against what's perceived as rising crime and disorder—as for instance among South Asians in Hounslow, who have this sense about new white asylum-seekers and travellers. But these are transitional problems that have occurred throughout the ages in dynamic cities like London. Maybe it's true in part of some of the northern mill towns, which have experienced some of the most acute racial tensions in recent years: witness Burnley, Oldham, Bradford. But we need to be specific in our analysis.

It's the same story with David Harvey—doom and gloom from start to finish: 'in certain times and places, the differences proliferate and intensify in negative and even pathological ways that inevitably sow seeds of civil strife'. But Harvey's lecture has a global dimension too: he also recognizes the significance of globalization (who doesn't, now?), and wants to remind us that the outcome isn't just advanced command and control centres such as London or New York, but also production cities such as 'Ciudad Juarez, Dacca, Shanghai, Seoul, Taipei, Hong Kong, Jakarta, Ho-Chi-Minh City, Manila, Bombay, and Bangalore, where the global sweatshops and degrading factory systems of a global capitalism grind away to produce my Gap shirts, Nike shoes, mechanical toys, and Sony Walkmans'. I am intrigued by this list, because I've visited quite a number of these cities, and I don't recognize his description of them: most are moving very rapidly in their turn to become command and control cities, and several (Hong Kong for instance) got there years ago.

For Harvey, as for Hall, it turns out that migration is bad news too, and for the same reason: it can result in 'bigotry and divisions, marginalizations and exclusions, sometimes boiling over into violent confrontations'. True, just like Hall, Harvey allows that some exciting mixing and fusing is taking place down there on some streets. But the overwhelming sense is that the whole system is grinding the faces of millions of poor people.

The reason, of course, is that Harvey hates the system.

The city is turned over to the growth machines, the financiers, the developers, the speculators, and the profiteers. The result is unnecessary deprivation (unemployment, housing shortages, and so on) in the midst of plenty. Hence the homeless on our streets and the beggars in the subways. Famines occur in the midst of food surpluses. Basic needs, like clean water, are denied to those who do not have the ability to pay. The excluded are forced to drink from cholera-infested rivers. This is what free markets actually do.

It's an apocalyptic picture of a city—any capitalist city. But which capitalist city, exactly? London? Tokyo? Singapore? Shanghai? Mexico City? Johannesburg? Some of the above, sure: a few beggars on a few streets, some presumably homeless; some unemployed, in those cities offering unemployment benefits (unemployment doesn't exist in poor countries; informal employment does, and that's a really important topic to discuss and dissect, but Harvey doesn't). Cholera-infested water? Well, we haven't heard much about cholera anywhere recently, because it's almost been eliminated. Various kinds of water-borne disease do exist, especially among children, and those are serious in some countries—though certainly not all.

Harvey, here as elsewhere, simply loses the point by failing to make any kind of distinction or differentiation between cities. They're all tarred with the same capitalist brush. And so we lead on to the inevitable Harveyan conclusion:

If this is where the inalienable rights of private property and the profit rate lead, then I want none of it. I am not alone in that conclusion. There is a huge movement for global justice that clearly sees the nature of the problem even as it struggles to identify viable alternatives [. . .] The right to the city is not a gift. It has to be seized by political movement.

I fear I won't be joining him on the barricades—and, more troubling, neither will almost anyone else. I just don't know where he's going to find all those fellow-fighters in this 'huge movement' of his. They're all too busy working assiduously to make it in the only system they know, which happens to be the capitalist system. That goes not only for Londoners and New Yorkers but also for Muscovites and Shanghaiers, who happen if old enough to have grown up in cities that once long ago were seized by such a political movement, only to see it crumble away of its own rottenness.

Richard Rogers's contribution is a very different kettle of fish, appearing almost bizarrely next door to these two latterday-Marxist diatribes. But his message will be equally familiar to all those well versed in the urban literature. It's equally apocalyptic in tone: it seems that these three contributors share a delight in doomery and gloomery, whatever the proximate cause that excites them. For Hall and Harvey, it's capitalism. For Rogers, it's suburbia. He really hates it:

A terrifying suburban sprawl threatens to destroy a significant proportion of the UK's precious countryside while simultaneously stripping inner cities of all vitality or direction. When people, shops, and jobs desert inner-city areas, the poor are left to inhabit ghost towns that are desolate, socially deprived, and fragmented. Many of our major cities are host to derelict and lifeless inner-city estates, shabby suburban sprawl, and dirty and squalid streets.

Again, faced with this positively Bladerunnerish account, I fell to wondering where exactly he had been lately. Presumably not his native London, since I cannot think of a single area that corresponds to it (except perhaps for one truly nightmarish estate in south-east London, which they are going to blow up any day now). Not even the great provincial cities such as Birmingham, Manchester, and Leeds, which are now staggering examples of urban renaissance that attract admiring professional visitors from abroad. Maybe, to be completely fair, some of the old one-industry towns surrounding these same core cities, which have lost their economic base and found it difficult or impossible to find another, and where people of different groups, white or black or brown, now face each other in equal unemployed glumness. But their problem isn't suburbia, theirs or anyone else's. It's that they've lost the reason for existence.

Perhaps, for some such cities, we ought to be thinking the unthinkable as they're now doing in some German cities: shrinking them to fit. But to blame it all on suburbia is simply to miss the analytical point. There are in fact two basic and quite different urban policy challenges in Britain, more specifically England, today, with quite different causes and requiring quite different solutions: there's a Southern problem, which is how to manage the Greater South East, one of the great polycentric megacity-regions of the world, and there's a Northern problem, which is how to repopulate or alternatively shrink parts of cities and towns in recognition of the fact that they've lost their economic rationale. Solving the first problem is going to require a massive increase in housebuilding to make up for a quite scandalous backlog brought about in part by earlier false analysis on the part of government and by the power of local NIMBY councils, and their electorates, to stop quite necessary development in order to protect their own charmed living standards. Much of this could and should go on brownfield land, including rural brownfield like old quarries and airfields, wherever such land is available; on that, everyone is agreed. But much will have to go on greenfield, unless English people are suddenly going to be willing to abandon their centuries-old preference for living in houses rather than flats.

And why should they? In what is still the best book on London ever written, nearly seventy years ago the Danish architect-planner Steen Eiler Rasmussen warned his readers against listening to siren architectural voices from continental Europe who would like to destroy the unique charm of their city by building over-high and over-dense.[1] His message was not heeded, and the high-rise disasters of the 1960s were the result. Rogers, it seems, is anxious that we should now finish the job.

He will doubtless argue that this is a travesty and that we can happily build good single-family housing at the densities of Islington or Chelsea. The problem with that is that even these houses, in many cases, do not accommodate the lifestyles and preferences of twenty-first-century English people: the multiple possessions, some of them bulky, the need for separate rooms for children to study or hang out, above all the cars. Yes, the cars: despite all attempts to persuade people to live a denser car-free style of life, most will reject it. So the campaign to get them all to live like Parisians or Milanese or Barcelonians is unlikely to work. It will just mean that those able to do so will buy older, bigger houses, forcing those unable to do so into smaller and more cramped and less suitable homes for them and their children.

The most problematic question about this campaign is exactly what it is for. It can't be to save land, because we have a huge surplus of agricultural land that is going to waste, and there are very large areas in every region—including the South East—that are of very indifferent scenic quality. It can't be to minimize long commuter journeys into London, because we learned sixty years ago how to do that by putting a green belt around the capital and planning so that growth of both jobs and people occurred in medium-sized towns well outside the normal commuting range. One is driven to the conclusion that it's to promote a particular kind of social engineering: to make people behave in ways that they wouldn't, left to their own devices:

A neighbourhood should have at least 5,000 people; that is about the minimum needed economically to support a bus, small shopping area, nursery, health clinic, and community hall. These focal areas should be within walking distance for all the inhabitants of the neighbourhood. A number of neighbourhoods makes a district, a number of districts adds up to a city centre, with each increase in scale supporting larger amenities. The city centre contains the Town Hall, university, cathedral, shopping centre, and so on.

All well and good, and what planning has been trying to achieve in these towns for half a century or more, with a good deal of success. But it doesn't need super-densities to achieve it: anything in the range of thirty to fifty dwellings per hectare will do it, while still achieving the kind of residential ambience that people evidently want. So why on earth deny them? And for what earthly reason propose, as Rogers does, to raise the brownfield ratio to '75 per cent in the first instance [. . .] a target of 100 per cent in many places if incentives and regulations were in place and properly enforced'? What is it all for?

Patrick Declerck's is a very different contribution from any of the three above: it is a closely observed account of what it actually means to be homeless in a city. Even though the homeless are far fewer in number than a critical commentator such as David Harvey suggests—generally, in a metropolis of the advanced world, they are a statistically negligible number—none the less they do inspire a disproportionate surge of sympathy on the part of the more fortunate majority: how could anyone come to this pass?

Declerck suggests that all the conventional and obvious explanations are wrong:

Chronic homelessness cannot be reduced to poverty, dereliction, or social exclusion. It is the madness of poverty, the madness of dereliction, the madness of social exclusion. It is, in a word, madness. And like all mad people, homeless people are very precious, both for the questions they raise and for the mockery they make of our aspirations. They show us the dark side of ourselves, the one that we do not want to be reminded of, the negative within us.

A psychiatrist who has worked with them, Declerck finds that many of them are 'past masters of regression'. Most have returned to the state of infants, and have to be treated as infants: ' "His Majesty the Baby", said Freud, to explain the demands that children place upon their parents. "His Majesty the Tramp" is the appropriate phrase here.' They live in worlds of their own: they are unable to maintain relationships with the rest of society, with everyday life, even with themselves. They live on the verge of breakdown. What sustains them, he says, is the elemental everyday fight for survival: 'It is a strange and paradoxical fact that, even though they seem to avoid all kinds of obligation, they live in a manner that obliges them to spend immense energy simply on surviving the next few hours.'

We can all resonate with that, because of course we all fight for survival: it is the existential condition. But for most of us, the fight is contained within what you could call Marquis of Queensberry rules, well understood and easy to follow through long routine: we get up, we travel to work through what can sometimes be horrible conditions, we maintain relationships with those we work with and for. And, as we know from accounts of life in wartime cities, to a remarkable degree life goes on even in conditions of extreme privation: recall Bill Brandt's immortal picture of the sleepers on the London tube, or the more harrowing pictures of lives in German cities towards the end of World War II, or in the Balkans more recently. But almost none of us struggles at this margin of existence day in, day out, as the homeless do.

Declerck reaches a remarkable and deeply disturbing conclusion: that we allow them to live like this because we cannot bring ourselves to recognize that the homeless are in fact mad.

It is of course the mad themselves who are made to pay the cost of that refusal. Society responds to the demands and needs of its life-long incapacitated members by judging that they had better run the risk of regrettable accidents such as rape, or death from hypothermia, than be accepted for who they are. It would be too threatening to our society if the homeless were allowed decent living conditions; we would rather they suffered.

But surely that conclusion goes far wider? There are other people on the streets of our cities who are not homeless but are evidently mad. Some are relatively harmless: they rant and rave and sing and talk to themselves or to the air. Some, sometimes, are far from harmless: they kill or rape or grievously harm other people. In one of the most fundamental revolutions in social behaviour of the last century, we emptied virtually all of these people out of the mental institutions in which they had previously been placed, putting them into something called 'community care'. Did it, does it work for them? Certainly, it gave them their freedom. But, on Declerck's analysis, that is like giving an infant freedom to roam the streets. It is fundamentally misconceived because it rests on the false premise that the mad are capable of being free like the rest of us.

Then there's Patricia Williams. A lawyer, she's very concerned with traditional Amnesty-type issues—in particular, the erosion of due legal process in her homeland, the United States, as the result of the so-called war on terrorism. I'm sure she's got a good point, worth a lecture; indeed, the Oxford Amnesty Lectures might consider borrowing this theme for a subsequent series. The only problem, for me, is that most of it isn't very centrally about cities, except in so far as most of us live in cities, so that everything about anything is city-relevant. She does have a specifically urban point later on, which is that city police tactics are becoming ever more like military operations, even to the point of calling in the army for help. She thinks that people in cities are buying into this because they're possessed by an overwhelming sense of fear.

The problem about this analysis, I think, is its Americocentricity—even, one might say, Newyorkcentricity. (In fairness, Williams does acknowledge this herself.) There's no doubt about its relevance there, as anyone can see who reads the flood of evidence coming out from America. But it doesn't accurately seem to describe what's happening in the rest of the urban world. There's been an enormous recent debate in the public prints about American exceptionalism. How far it exists is a debatable subject. But no one can doubt, surely, that the American response to 9/11 was unique, the reaction of a country that had never experienced serious urban terrorism before. And in New York, for obvious reasons, it reached fever pitch. In European capitals, above all London, we've lived with this kind of thing for years. It's almost horrible to say that you learn to live with it, but you do. You get it into perspective and you learn to get on with your life. You do have debates, as we're having in the UK every day, about extending the powers of the police and of the prosecutors in dealing with allegations of terrorism and related subjects—some of them very distantly related, as defenders of freedom are not slow to point out. But some sense of perspective is needed.

Finally, there's James Wolfensohn. Again, he starts from an entirely different place from the others. He has a different question, an economist's question: how do we make poor people richer? At the World Bank, which he heads, they decided that they didn't really know what poverty was. So they asked the poor: 60,000 of them in sixty countries. And they received a funny answer: the poor didn't first and foremost complain about lack of money. That might be because most of them don't use money much. What they do want is to be heard, to be recognized, to be free from fear, to have the opportunity to climb out of poverty, and not to be hungry. Women, in particular, stressed freedom from fear and from gender persecution. What the poor want most deeply is to make something of their own lives as human beings. They want the chance to work to make lives better for themselves and their children. They're just like the rest of us. And they want to do it themselves. They don't want charity, though they may need help.

Wolfensohn tells the story of a poor slum woman in Brazil who brought up her children as a lone mother. She made all her children stay on at school until they passed their courses, never allowing them to give up. 'I raised all my children amid drugs, robbery, cocaine, marijuana, and crack, but thanks to God none of them ever got involved with these things,' she says. 'For a poor mother living in a *favela* with many sons, it is a victory.' All are at work and studying to enter university.

The first essential for Wolfensohn, if the poor are to help lever themselves up, is good government, fair regulations, impartial and effective administration, a legal and judicial framework that protects their rights, financial systems that work, and a civil society that is free from corruption. All that, to veteran Marxists such as Hall or Harvey, might seem typical of the grip of global capitalism on the World Bank and similar institutions. But stop and consider: where, today, do we find the most grinding poverty and total lack of freedom, especially for women? Precisely in those failed states, overwhelmingly in sub-Saharan Africa and the Middle East, that lack virtually all these basic elements. Where do we find things problematic but getting better? Precisely in those Latin American countries that failed on many of these counts a quarter century ago, but have got spectacularly better. And where do we find the most stupendous progress in reducing poverty? Precisely in those Asian Pacific countries that, though still imperfect in important respects, have made the greatest progress in providing good governance.

Beyond these basics, says Wolfensohn, the poor above else need a decent education system, health care, infrastructure, and access to secure housing. How to achieve these things will vary from one country to another, depending on history and culture. Too right: I've long been fascinated to notice, for instance, how there's a Latin American model of development and a Pacific Asian one. The first stresses informal approaches: go easy on popular land occupations and then go in and provide the services; leave it to private enterprise to develop informal bus-based transport systems. The second stresses central welfare provision: public housing at high density with supporting mass transit systems. Yet both appear to work, and if you look at two of the outstandingly successful cases of urban development in the world, celebrated in all the articles—Singapore and Curitiba—you find that behind the apparent differences there are very similar outcomes.

That's important, because Wolfensohn convincingly shows that the great challenge is going to be the growth of slums in the cities of the developing world. Whatever the approach here, the real revolution in the past thirty years has been in the mindsets of those who run these cities—the politicians and the bureaucrats. They now understand that they have to serve all their citizens, not just the fortunate few. It's a revolution rather like the one that extended the vote in nineteenth-century cities and countries.

The key to successful policy, already evident from scores of successful examples in cities across Asia and Latin America, is to give poor people the tools to upgrade their own housing in their own neighbourhoods. That means:

installing or improving basic infrastructure such as water, waste collection, and electricity; mitigating the threat of environmental disaster; improving access to health care and education; supporting programmes that protect citizens against crime and violence; constructing community facilities such as nurseries, health posts, and open spaces; regularizing security of tenure; enhancing income-earning opportunities through training and micro-credit; and building the institutional framework to sustain improvements.

Self-help, then: something the Marxists would dismiss as a capitalist plot, but one that has been proven to work, again and again, in countless cases around the world. Most importantly, it depends on giving slum dwellers the security and stability that will cause them to make the effort to invest in their own neighbourhoods. That means giving them security of tenure. As Wolfensohn puts it, 'it says to the urban poor: "you have a right to remain in the place you call home." '

Wolfensohn is adamant, and doubtless controversial, when he goes on to argue that security of tenure is far more import- ant than money. The statistics, he argues, show that every dollar invested by the authorities in slum upgrading yields no less than seven dollars of investment from residents. So it's not true that the poor have no money: they have some, and besides they have the sweat equity of their own labour. He tells a significant story from Brazil:

Many of the women I met during my trip to the *favelas* in Rio were keen to present me with the receipt proving that they had paid their water bill. What they were in fact showing me was the first official document that bore their names. Having such a document meant that they could go down into Rio and buy a bicycle or apply for a bank loan because, for the first time in their lives, they could offer proof of address. It meant that they were, all of a sudden, recognized members of society.

There's room here for informed debate, without doubt: debate about just how much money the rest of us, including richer nations, need to invest in this process so as to unlock all this potential among the urban poor themselves. The radicals will argue that benign neglect is not in itself enough. But what cannot be doubted by anyone who cares to look at the over- whelming empirical evidence is that Wolfensohn is right, and the point he's making is far and away the truest and most important argument of this entire collection: *the new development paradigm works*. It has the potential to raise billions out of poverty into a secure and dignified life. And above all it does so by giving them freedom: the most basic freedom of all, to shape their own lives.

That, rather than carping on the iniquities of global capitalism, is the only path worth following. But I don't expect to persuade the unpersuaded. Nor should they expect to persuade me or the many serious students of urbanism, James Wolfensohn notable among them, who think likewise.

Oxonian Epilogue

Patrick Declerck

At the invitation of the Sunday Times Oxford Literary Festival, I went back to Oxford in April 2005 to participate in a debate on homelessness with John Bird, founder of the *Big Issue*. During the discussion, I was asked what I thought of ASBOs. I had no idea what an ASBO was, and someone kindly explained that the acronym stood for Anti-Social Behaviour Order. I said I was instinctively wary of any measure pertaining to such a vague and intrinsically dangerous notion as that of anti-social behaviour.

After the debate, a woman resident of Oxford came up to me and thrust a leaflet into my hands. 'This is what an ASBO looks like,' she said. 'I received this one in my post-box. It concerns a woman who lives in my neighbourhood. It's terrible that things have come to this.' What she had given me was a leaflet folded three ways. I have it next to me as I write. On the first page, under the inch-high letters ASBO, is a 3-inch by 2½-inch photograph, says the caption, of one Jennifer Ford, age 44, of Whitehouse Road. Jennifer Ford's head is tilted towards the camera. Her face stares out at us with a slightly bemused look. The general effect is not unlike someone straining to distinguish something through the murky waters of an aquarium.

'Keeping crime off our streets' (white letters on blue background with the word 'crime' in—you'll never guess—red) blares the legend at the bottom of the page. Grateful citizens owe this gallant attempt at social control to two institutional bodies who advertise their own names three times. One is Oxford City Council's Crime and Nuisance Action Team (CANAct for short, and we certainly hope the pun is duly appreciated because, by God, Madam, such good wordplay stuff is not easy to come by and took a bit of brain exertion to come up with, I can tell you). The other is something pleasantly called 'Together Oxford'. There's a bit of dry humour there, of course, because, I mean, Oxford is not quite absolutely together, is it now? Not quite together with, say, the likes of Jennifer Ford, that blot on the landscape, for instance, eh?

Precisely.

If we go ahead and open up this leaflet, what do we find? Well, just in case we had missed it the first time around, we are confronted with the same photograph of the same woman wearing the same lost look. And we learn the following:

This is Jennifer Ford who lives on Whitehouse Road. She has been made the subject of an Anti-Social Behaviour Order, until 29 March 2007. She risks arrest and could be jailed if she breaches this order. She must not act in an anti-social way anywhere within Riverside Court, part of Salter Close, streets or parts of, namely, Worcester St, Beaumont St, Gloucester St, Broad St, Castle St, High St, Queen St and New Road.

Then, under five headings:

What She Did . . .
- Smashed neighbours' windows
- Used abusive language in the area she lives
- Caused a nuisance by shouting in public
- Drunken behaviour on numerous occasions in public

The Result

The courts have made an Anti-Social Behaviour Order (ASBO) against Jennifer Ford until March 2007, which states that she is prohibited from:

- Entering Riverside Court and part of Salter Close;
- Entering streets or part of streets, namely, Worcester Street, Beaumont Street, Gloucester Street, George Street, Broad Street, Castle Street, High Street, Queen Street and New Road;
- Carrying a knife or other bladed instrument without lawful authority or reasonable excuse in a public place;
- Using threatening, abusive or insulting words or behaviour in Whitehouse Road, or instructing or encouraging any other person to do so.

What You Can DO

If Jennifer Ford breaches her ASBO, she risks arrest and custody. You can report any breach to St Aldate's Police Station and Oxford City Council (phone numbers on back page)—safe in the knowledge that you are helping to protect your community.

The Future

Jennifer Ford is now suffering the consequences of her own anti-social behaviour. If others behave in a threatening, alarming or distressing way we should work together to stop them and to make a safer neighbourhood for ourselves and our children.

By getting involved and having the courage to speak out, we can make individuals like Jennifer Ford accountable for their actions.

Help to improve your community and take back control.

Your Safety Comes First

When you call us on the numbers on the back page, we promise to investigate promptly on what you tell us—about Jennifer Ford or others who behave in an anti-social way.

We are ready with the support you need to help us bring offenders to court.

The back page lists the phone numbers of the Anti-Social Behaviour Actionline, something called 'Crime Stoppers', and the police. It seductively invites citizens to 'call us with confidence—in confidence. Let's refuse to accept crime and anti-social behaviour in our area.'

To summarize, what we have here is a female member of the underclass, most probably an alcoholic, who occasionally rants and raves and curses and who, at least once, broke a neighbour's window. For these 'crimes' she is publicly denounced, stigmatized, and humiliated in her neighbourhood, a neighbourhood which she almost certainly cannot afford to leave; for the same 'crimes' she is, for two years, susceptible to be investigated at any time on the pretext of anonymous denunciations by anyone; anonymous denunciations that are both solicited and encouraged. The rationale behind this measure is called Naming and Shaming. The mechanism of the naming may be obvious, but methinks the shame lies in the very concept of the measure rather than in the alleged 'crimes' it purports to control.

As to the nature of those 'crimes', one does not need to be a legal expert to sense that there is something very wrong in the way they are here defined. It would seem that either an act is illegal or it is not. If it is, then, all things being equal, it should be prosecuted. If it is not, then from a judicial point of view, there is nothing more to say. It appears that ASBOs refuse the very principle of this basic dichotomy and that the notion of anti-social behaviour itself covers a spectrum of acts and attitudes that stretches vertiginously from the reprehensible to the absolutely banal. Smashing a neighbour's window is clearly reprehensible. Being drunk is banal. So is cursing. And what does 'being a nuisance' mean, exactly? Of the various charges listed, the strangest of all is that she 'used abusive language in the area she lives'. Is using abusive language in itself reprehensible? And if it is, what does the location one is in when one uses abusive language have to do with the 'crime' of using abusive language? Are we, surrealistically, to understand that the use of abusive language is reprehensible in the area one lives in, but not elsewhere? How far, pray, must one walk from one's home before being allowed to give blasphemous vent to one's feelings? Going back to the text of the leaflet one sees that this is precisely the kind of absurd legal and logical cleft stick to which the system is driven by the very sloppiness of this ill-thought measure. Apart from any other humanitarian, ethical, or political consideration, and only from the point of view of the strict logic of any legal system, one measures the inherently terrifying arbitrariness that underlies such judicial orders as being forbidden to 'act in an anti-social way anywhere within Riverside Court and part of Salter Close'. Please, Sir, is outside Riverside Court OK? Or is it all right if I stay away from Salter Close altogether? Could the same behaviour, the same acts, the same 'crimes' indulged in and committed half a mile from one another lead in one case to imprisonment, in another to a fine, in yet another to nothing more than the general reprobation and eyebrow raising of devout elderly ladies and fine upstanding moustached gentlemen? Could this be justice? Or is this whole apparatus of legal, social, and ideological control merely the flimsy and all too transparent mask of class justice, of class repression, of class vengeance?

Oh no? Pushing it, am I? Egalitarian, is it? The same for everyone, cross my heart and hope to die? The fundamental principle of justice, that which states that all are equal before the law, is preserved; the cornerstone that first and foremost distinguishes justice from arbitrary vengeance. Untouched, unsullied by such practices? Really? Let us dare ask, then, a few unsavoury questions. Does Tony Blair have an ASBO slapped on him for leading the country into a war under false pretences and paper-thin pretexts? What about Prince Harry, for dressing up as a Nazi? After all, there, undoubtedly, is anti-social behaviour par excellence. Will corporate executives be made the subject of ASBOs for bankrupting their companies and ruining people's lives through their greed, delusions of grandeur, stupidity, and incompetence, as happens every day? Yes or no? Poor, misguided, Jennifer Ford! How sadly pitiful, amateurish, and silly her dabblings into anti-social behaviour patterns seem. Little does she know . . .

And what about me? Do I not deserve an ASBO against me too? For unfortunate but incontrovertible evidence has it, gentle reader, that I have not been above abusing the blushful Hippocrene myself from time to time. As to the use of language that would meet with pursed lips in the foc'sle of one of the more disreputable of pirate ships, I do not like to boast, but I am practically a professional; indeed, I hardly think it possible for one to produce anything of a literary nature without sustaining oneself through evanescent inspiration and tricky paragraphs with a steady stream of red-hot epithets and metaphors of a generally anatomical nature. Perhaps it would be best not to wait meekly for the ultimate and inevitable detection or denunciation, but to beat them to it, and, in melancholy solidarity with the Jennifer Fords of this world, gravely and proudly to sign:

Yours truly,

Patrick Declerck ASBO (Oxon. Hon.)

(who invites you, gentle reader, to do the same).

Endnotes

Introduction

1. Michel de Montaigne, *The Complete Works*, trans. Donald M. Frame (London: Everyman's Library, 2003), 'Essays', iii. 5, p. 903 (translation modified).
2. UN-Habitat, *The Challenge of Slums: Global Report on Human Settlements 2003* (2003).
3. Matthew Gibney (ed.), *Globalizing Rights: The Oxford Amnesty Lectures 1999* (Oxford: Oxford University Press, 2003).
4. Kate E. Tunstall (ed.), *Displacement, Asylum, Migration: The Oxford Amnesty Lectures 2004* (forthcoming from Oxford University Press).
5. See *A. v. Secretary of State for the Home Department* [2004] UKHL 56.
6. See Annan's Foreword to the UN-Habitat report, *The Challenge of Slums*, quoted above.

Note to Introduction to Chapter 1

1. 'The Formation of a Diasporic Intellectual', interview with Kuan-Hsing Chen, in *Stuart Hall: Critical Dialogues in Cultural Studies* (London: Routledge, 1996).

Notes to Chapter 1

1. See Stuart Hall, 'The Multicultural Question', in Barnor Hesse, *Un/settled Multiculturalisms* (London: Zed Books, 2000).

2. See Saskia Sassen, *The Global City* (Princeton, NJ: Princeton University Press, 1996).

3. Gary Bridge and Sophie Watson, 'City Economies', in eid. (eds.), *A Companion to the City* (Oxford: Blackwell, 2002), 255.

4. See David Harvey, *The Condition of Postmodernity* (Oxford: Blackwell, 1989).

5. See Francis Fukuyama, *The End of History and the Last Man* (Harmondsworth: Penguin, 1992).

6. Michael Hardt and Antonio Negri, *Empire* (Harvard, Mass.: Harvard University Press, 2000).

7. See Philip Bobbitt, *The Shield of Achilles* (Harmondsworth: Penguin, 2002).

8. See Stuart Hall, 'Labour's Double Shuffle', in *Soundings*, 24 (2003).

9. The *Guardian*, 5 November 2003.

10. A. Kundani, 'From Oldham to Bradford: The Violence of the Violated', *Race and Class*, 43 (2001).

11. Herman Ouseley, *Community Pride Not Prejudice*, Report to Bradford City Council (2001).

12. Ash Amin, *Ethnicity and the Multicultural City* (London: Economic and Social Research Council, 2002).

13. Bhikhu Parekh (ed.), *The Parekh Report: The Future of Multi-Ethnic Britain* (London: Profile Books, 2000), 27.

14. Les Back, *New Ethnicities and Urban Culture* (London: UCL Press, 1996).

15. Ash Amin, 'The Economic Base of Contemporary Cities', in G. Bridge and S. Watson (eds.), *A Companion to the City* (Oxford: Blackwell, 2002), 9.

16. Bridge and Watson, 'City Economies'.

17. See Hall, 'The Multicultural Question'.

18. A more detailed account of this development in the US—and of its effect on policing and justice in American cities—is offered by Patricia Williams in the next chapter of this book.

Notes to Chapter 2

1. 'Rumsfeld's Remarks Anger DC Officials', *The Washington Post* (20 June 2003), B1.

2. Sacvan Bercovitch, *The American Jeremiad* (Madison: University of Wisconsin Press, 1978).

3. 'Ashcroft Defends Detention As Immigrants Recount Toll', *New York Times* (5 June 2003), A21.

4. 'Teen Arrested at Logan for Alleged Bomb Threat in his Bag', *The Boston Globe* (2 August 2003).

5. Jacobo Timerman, *Prisoner Without a Name, Cell Without a Number*, trans. Toby Talbot (London: Weidenfeld & Nicolson, 1993); Pierre Vidal-Naquet, *La Torture dans la République* (Paris: Maspero, 1983).

6. Arthur Miller, *The Crucible* (New York: Viking Press, 1971), Act 1, p. 34.

Notes to Chapter 3

1. Robert Park, *On Social Control and Collective Behavior* (Chicago: Chicago University Press, 1967), 3.

2. Henri Lefebvre, *Writings on Cities* (Oxford: Blackwell, 1996), 158.

3. See Jeremy Seabrook, *In the Cities of the South: Scenes from a Developing World* (London: Verso, 1996).

4. Karl Marx, *Capital* (New York: International Publishers, 1967), i. 225.

5. See Henri Lefebvre, *The Urban Revolution* (Minneapolis: Minnesota University Press, 2003).

6. Marx, *Capital*, i. 174.

7. See David Harvey, *Spaces of Hope* (Edinburgh: Edinburgh University Press, 2001).

8. Louis Marin, *Utopics: Spatial Play* (London: Macmillan, 1984).

9. Lefebvre, *The Urban Revolution*; Michel Foucault, 'Of Other Spaces', *Diacritics*, 16 (1986), 22–7.

10. On this see Harvey, *Spaces of Hope*, ch. 8.

11. Lefebvre, *Writings on Cities*, 149.

12. A statement of this view is offered by James Wolfensohn in the next chapter of this book.

13. Plato, *Republic* (Harmondsworth: Penguin, 1955), 66.

14. On this see Michael Walzer, *Spheres of Justice: A Defence of Pluralism and Equality* (Oxford: Blackwell, 1983).

15. See Michel Foucault, 'On Popular Justice: A Discussion with Maoists', in *Power/Knowledge*, ed. C. Gordon (London: Harvester Wheatsheaf, 1980).

16. John Rawls, *A Theory of Justice* (Cambridge, Mass.: Harvard University Press, 1971).

17. See David Harvey, *The New Imperialism* (Oxford: Oxford University Press, 2003).

18. On this see Don Mitchell, *The Right to the City* (Minneapolis: Minnesota University Press, 2003); see also Patrick Declerck's contribution to this volume.

19. This is the subject of Harvey, *The New Imperialism*.

20. George W. Bush, 'Securing Freedom's Triumph', *New York Times* (11 September 2002), A33.

21. Seabrook, *In the Cities of the South*, 103.

22. See Harvey, *The New Imperialism*, ch. 4.

23. See the World Bank's World Development Report for 2000–1, *Attacking Poverty* (Washington, DC: World Bank, 2000).

24. See, for example, Walden Bello, *Deglobalization: Ideas for a New World* (London: Zed Books, 2002); John Cavanagh *et al.* (eds.), *Alternatives to Economic Globalization* (San Francisco: Bennett-Koehler, 2002); and Barry Gills (ed.), *Globalization and the Politics of Resistance* (New York: Palgrave, 2001).

25. Henri Saint-Simon, *Selected Writings on Science, Industry, and Social Organization* (London: Croom Helm, 1975), 162–8, 227–8.

26. Mitchell, *The Right to the City*, 129.

27. Quoted in David Harvey, *Justice, Nature, and the Geography of Difference* (Oxford: Blackwell, 1996), 439.

Notes to Chapter 4

1. See http://ddp-ext.worldbank.org/ext/MDG/home.do (accessed 27 July 2005) for further details.

2. See http://www1.worldbank.org/prem/poverty/voices (accessed 27 July 2005).

3. What follows is based on Deepa Narayan and Patti Petesch (eds.), *Voices of the Poor: From Many Lands* (New York: Oxford University Press for the World Bank, 2002).

4. *Cities Alliance for Cities Without Slums* (The World Bank and UNCHS (Habitat), Special Summary Edition, 1999), 1.

5. For further information see *Cities Alliance for Cities Without Slums* (1999), 2–9.

6. The United Nations Millennium Declaration, Resolution A/RES/55/2, paragraph 19 (Target 11).

7. See *Cities Alliance for Cities Without Slums: 2002 Annual Report*, 24–7.

8. See Alain Durand-Lasserve *et al.*, 'Secure Tenure for the Urban Poor', Cities Alliance *CIVIS*, 3 (2002).

9. A similar institution in Mexico is called *Mi Casa* ('my home'). See http://www.micasa.gob.mx (accessed 22 June 2005) for further details.

10. Narayan and Petesch (eds.), *Voices of the Poor*, 364.

Note to Chapter 5

1. Richard Rogers, *Cities for a Small Planet* (London: Faber & Faber, 1997).

Notes to Chapter 6

1. George Orwell, *Down and Out in Paris and London* (Harmondsworth: Penguin Books, 1940).

2. Herman Melville, 'Bartleby', in *Billy Budd, Sailor and Other Stories* (Harmondsworth: Penguin Classics, 1985).

3. See, for instance, the collective work *Pouvoirs du négatif dans la psychanalyse et la culture* (Seyssel: Champ Vallon, 1988).

4. Ministère de l'emploi et de la solidarité, Direction des affaires sanitaires et sociales de Paris, Protocole Grand Froid 2001/2002, 30 October 2001. The translation is mine.

5. Donald Winnicott, *Playing and Reality* (London: Tavistock, 1971).

6. Arthur Schopenhauer, *On the Freedom of the Will* (New York: Library of Liberal Arts, Bobbs–Merrill, 1960).

7. Ludwig Wittgenstein, *Tractatus Logico-Philosophicus* (London: Routledge & Kegan Paul, 1971).

8. William Shakespeare, *The Tempest*, v. i.

Notes to Chapter 7

Research for this Response was undertaken with the support of the Arts and Humanities Research Board. I would like also to thank Richard A. Falk, Andrew Harding, Joy Mooberry, and David Sugarman.

1. See M. B. Likosky (ed.), *Privatising Development: Transnational Law, Infrastructure, and Human Rights* (Leiden: Brill, 2005); M. B. Likosky, *The Silicon Empire: Law, Culture, and Commerce* (Aldershot: Ashgate, 2005).

2. See (among others) T. Carothers, *Aiding Democracy Abroad: The Learning Curve* (Washington, DC: Carnegie, 1999); J. Faundez (ed.), *Good Government and Law: Legal and Institutional Reform in Developing Countries* (London: Macmillan, 1997); M. B. Likosky (ed.), *Transnational Legal Processes: Globalization and Power Disparities* (London: Butterworths, 2002); W. Twining, *Globalization and Legal Theory* (London: Butterworths, 2000).

3. On the different forms of privatization see M. M. Brown, 'Privatization: A Foretaste of the Book', in M. M. Brown and

G. Ridley (eds.), *Privatization: Current Issues* (London: Graham & Trotman, 1994), p. xv. For a treatment focusing on the nuances of privatization see C. G. Veljanovski, *Selling the State: Privatization in Britain* (London: Weidenfeld & Nicolson, 1987).

4. On BOT contracts see Likosky (ed.), *Privatising Development*. See also D. A. Levy 'BOT and Public Procurement: A Conceptual Framework', *Indiana International and Comparative Law Review*, 7 (1996), 95; S. M. Levy, *Build, Operate, Transfer: Paving the Way for Tomorrow's Infrastructure* (New York: John Wiley & Sons, 1996); United Nations Industrial Development Organization, *UNIDO BOT Guidelines* (Vienna: UNIDO, 1996).

Note to Chapter 8

1. S. E. Rasmussen, *London: The Unique City* (London: Jonathan Cape, 1937).

Index